Alien

Encounters

Human Encounters With Ufos and Extraterrestrials

(The Untold Story of Alien Contact During the Apollo Moon Landing)

Walter Thurston

Published By **Kate Sanders**

Walter Thurston

Alien Encounters: Human Encounters With Ufos and Extraterrestrials (The Untold Story of Alien Contact During the Apollo Moon Landing)

ISBN 978-1-7770736-8-8

Table Of Contents

No part of this guidebook shall be reproduced in any form without permission in writing from the publisher except in the case of brief quotations embodied in critical articles or reviews.

Legal & Disclaimer

The information contained in this book is not designed to replace or take the place of any form of medicine or professional medical advice. The information in this book has been provided for educational & entertainment purposes only.

The information contained in this book has been compiled from sources deemed reliable, and it is accurate to the best of the Author's knowledge; however, the Author cannot guarantee its accuracy and validity and cannot be held liable for any errors or omissions. Changes are periodically made to this book. You must consult your doctor or get professional medical advice before using any of the suggested remedies, techniques, or information in this book.

Chapter 1: Betty And Barney Hill

Two people, on their way home from a pleasant vacation in the month of September, 1961 were ripped apart by a horrific encounter. Betty (41) as well as Barney (39) was traveling on Route 3 within New Hampshire, near Indian Head. The time was around 10:15pm. when they noticed a large colorful, large and multi-colored pancake form at the top of the sky. They observed it with more curiosity than fear as their car stopped and the object appeared to bind them on the road. With his firearm as well as his binoculars Barney took off from the vehicle to investigate the object. Barney said he saw around 10-11 tiny humans in the machine and through two windows. The two of them both heard what appeared to be a kind of buzzing sound. Another thing that they remembers...is getting home two hours late than they ought to have! In spite of the missed time the couple did not think to anyone the possibility of being taken away.

The next couple of evenings, Betty started having recurring nightmares about being entangled in the bizarre structure that they had seen. Both of them did not feel particularly healthy or refreshed, which is what they would've expected following some time off.

To find out the reason They both went through the same regressive hypnosis procedure, however as the bizarre story of their first encounter with aliens from the USA was revealed.

The aliens took the victims into their spacecraft and examined them medically, and very closely, but not in a rough manner. Betty recalls feeling pain when an extremely long needle was placed into her navel. Barney confessed, reluctantly to having provided a sample of semen.

They were both interviewed multiple times throughout the years, and each time separately, but they did not have any contradictions in their descriptions. Both of them described the creature being about 5 feet tall having grey skins with huge, large head-shaped pear heads that have an angled, cat-like eye.

One of the most remarkable aspects of the event is Betty claims she was shown a map was calling an "star-map" by one of the aliens that wanted to know whether she was able to pinpoint which location they were in the map. Betty could not accomplish this, however she was able to recall sufficient information from the map that she was able to draw it after the influence of hypnosis. The "star-map" created a massive outrage as numerous renowned researchers have produced long reports, delving into the map with great detail, concluding that it has many similarities to other locations within the universe. It is known as being the Zeta Reticuli system of stars as well as the revered journal "Astronomy" was the first to publish a detailed debate on the subject in 1974.

The couple is educated, but it's amazing to see that Betty terrified and shaking like she was and unable to remember the details of the incredibly complex "star Map". However, she could draw maps from her memory, which professional experts took seriously. The evidence that supports the claims of Hill is the evidence it is the Project Blue Book, officially maintained by the Air Force at that time records a evidence of a UFO in the night, from two sites in the area.

Chapter 2: Betty Andreasson

It was a night like one other. Betty prepared a meal for her entire family with 7 kids. The parents of her mother and father were in her home at the time because her husband was admitted to the hospital. They were in the kitchen at her house situated in South Ashburham, Massachusetts at approximately 6:30 pm on the 25th of February 1967. The light fixtures in the home were suddenly dim and then the house was lit by a reddish orange light emanating from the backyard. As Betty ran to comfort her kids, her father was astonished to witness 5 odd looking people exiting the craft area and scurry toward the house...coming directly through the doors!

Everybody, with the exception of Betty appeared to be in the Trance. Before she had time to get scared the head of the group, a bit higher than the rest and taller than the others, spoke to Betty by telepathically. Betty was able to understand the alien's message and was able to understand it even though its mouth, which looked like a cut within his huge pear-shaped skull was still in place. The aliens were dressed in blue one-piece overalls, with large belts, and birds-like symbols on their sleeves. Even though they were wearing boots however, they never touched the ground, but gliding instead of walking. They appeared friendly and she was sure that her family was safe so she gladly accompany them on their way to the spaceship. A single alien was still in the home.

Within the four hours following, she went through an array of bizarre events. Her body was examined and an implant of a smaller size was taken from her head through the nose. They took her to a second section of the ship in which she was able to see even more bizarre creature in red, who began by submerging her into the gray liquid that was then flushed away. Then she had a image of a massive creature being smoldering to the point of the ground and then rising again in the form of the appearance of a Phoenix ascending. She was very blessed and joyful and was overwhelmed by a feeling of religious awe.

Her return was safe back to her home and her entire family was freed from their slumber and settled down to sleep normal. On the next day, they faintly thought they had been visited by bizarre entities that didn't pose any threat. They appeared to be able of floating through the doors, and were then surrounded by an orange, reddish color.

The normal routine continued in the aftermath of this traumatic incident. As a committed Christian, Betty survived a divorce and later the disappearance of her husband as in addition to the tragedy of losing her youngest children in a crash. The life of Betty took a brighter turn when she was married and met Bob Luca. The wedding took place 10 years following the visit of an alien that the incident once more was a major factor in her life.

Betty was able to discover, when she went through the regressive method of hypnosis that she was actually involved in several alien experiences during her lifetime, beginning around the age of four years old. She was not only capable of recalling, while under an hypnotic state, details from at the very least four incidents, but she also could describe an alien being, Quazgaa who was a close acquaintance. It was even more fascinating, as it seemed that her spouse, Bob, as well as her daughter Becky weren't strangers to encounters with aliens. The writer Raymond Fowler has written 5 books that provide an extremely thorough account of these encounters.

Most of the memories she recalls involve an intense feeling of devotional fervor. The descriptions she gives of her experiences often seem more like "near-death moments" that hint at the joy that comes with being freed from physical connection to a state of spiritual bliss and not encounters with other beings. A majority of Christian fundamentalists equate contact with aliens with a very negative energies, which bridge the spiritual.

Such contradictions have did not seem to have any effect on Betty Andreasson Luka.

Chapter 3: Herbert Schirmer

The Patrolman Herbert Schirmer looked at the report he'd written for the 3rd December of 1967. Training was a way of ensuring that he was exact about all incidents that took place during his time, and that was exactly what happened. "Saw an aircraft flying at the intersection of highways 63 and 6. You'll be amazed!" At about 2am in the morning, while on a routine patrol along the edge of the tiny village in Ashland in Nabraska He had observed some red lights flashing in the roadway and went to look into. When he got closer to the location, it became apparent that there was something that looked like an disc, floating around 8 feet high above the road. While he was watching the object, a landing "legs" emerged and then the metal object fell. He noticed that the car he was driving to the target and saw that the entire structure was enclosed by a cat-walk which was just beneath a line of windows that were oval.

A bright white light glowed under the craft's surface after a hatch slid open, and two figures resembling humanoids slipped away and headed towards Herb's vehicle. The first figure stopped right near the car and seemed to spray the vehicle with a fine, green mist. The second figure walked through the window that was open at the side of the driver. The person seemed to be friendly, and placed a small silver piece of jewellery to Herbs neck, right below the left ears. The figure asked "Are you the watchman in this location?" Herb said "Yes Sir" and the person said "Watchman I'm coming with you". What followed, Herb thought of was the vision of an orange and reddish light emerging from the craft, and then it soaring off. It was followed by a loud siren sound.

The next morning, Herb was ill and suffering from an intense headache. Also, he developed a nasty skin blemish around his neck. The incident caused quite a stir within the small town, and there was no time before Herb was questioned through The Gordon Committee from the University of Colorado. In regressive hypnosis, Herb remembers what transpired when he followed the person to the lair, with incredible specific way.

He was shown the three levels of the vessel and was able to draw intricate drawings of the interior along with the manner of propulsion that was described as "reversible electromagnetic force".

The group was between 4 and 5 feet tall. They were dressed in silver grey uniforms, with an emblem of a winged snake embroidered across right breast. They wore long, thin heads that had rather round noses, and mouths that resembled slits. The skin was grey/white shade and the eyes of the cat were not blinking. The occupants wore helmets and gloves equipped with an antenna that was small in the left right ear. Herb believed that it was part of their communications system.

Though he was able to comprehend the bulk of their language, Herb felt that he couldn't always understand the meaning of the information that he received. The location they originated using a star map that which he couldn't comprehend and was informed that they "had a base in Venus". The chief claimed that one of the reasons of visiting Earth was to obtain electricity from the sources of electricity in earth...then they demonstrated exactly how they did this through tapping into a power grid in the vicinity, possibly one of the reasons they arrived at this particular location.

When the excitement gone and the craze had slowed, Herb returned to his job at Ashland. In the following months, He was elevated to Chief of Police. It didn't work very well for him. the smug local residents kept making fun of his name and the car was dynamited in an joke. Unfortunately, the pressure was excessive for his wife to leave the relationship. One of his regressive sessions Herb mentions that aliens informed him that they will see them two times during his lifetime time and "he could see the entire universe".

Chapter 4: The Buff Ledge Camp Abduction

In the afternoon two young workers at the summer camp at Lake Champlain in Vermont, were relaxing and taking in the views of the lake from their docks for boats.

Michael Lapp (16) and Janet Cornell (19) noticed an intense light, visible on the horizon, heading towards them. They quickly realized they were looking at an air craft that was a kind of craft and were astonished at how three tiny lights separated their craft from its main. They began to carry out what could be described as flight patterns that were choreographed across the sky. Then the aircraft appeared to plunge right into the lake. It then came back up following, and then glide across the lake towards those watching in shock. Michael saw clearly two persons within the craft, and exclaimed with a slap on his leg. The other figure mimicked this action and, as the craft sped up to overhead and erupted a glowing beam. Michael was able to feel a floating feeling at first, and then suddenly fearful of being kidnapped, yelled out; "No, we don't wish to join the others". He then recalls is that he was seated together with Janet whom he believed to be lost in thought sitting on the dock of the boat when"the "mother craft" was sunk into the dim night sky.

They did not discuss the incident. They each went on their own. Michael was unable to think about it every now and again however, after a few years, he became severely afflicted with migraines and a lack of sleep. He reached out to Walter Webb, a UFO specialist, and he suggested the regressive hypnotism technique could help with the ailments.

After being hypnotized for 10 years of being hypnotized, Michael could recall the exact events that occurred to Michael as well as Janet like it had happened the previous day. If Janet was located and consented to undergo tests, she verified everything Michael was saying, before she had even heard any of his words.

They both were taken to the small craft, and then transferred to a bigger ship. Both were thoroughly examined and the doctor watched them as Janet laid on the table. Little creatures shined lights in Janet's eyes. They scraped the skin off her face and then drew the body fluids. Janet recalls feeling extremely cold and cold after having hair pulled back and neck squeezed.

The aliens claimed they wanted to "make the world look as ours...other destinations" Michael remembers. All of them had similar appearances. One of the most striking features was their huge, nearly wrapped around eyes, and mouths with no lips. The necks of their subjects were length and had no hair. Their noses were just tiny holes and did not appear to have any ears. Michael was able to see three pointed, web-like fingers in each hand, and their bodies seemed humid and sticky when touched.

While hypnotized the two do not seem to retain any memories of when they got back to the deck of their boat following the disappearance. Later, it was discovered that some of the camp, returning after an excursion, had actually seen a mysterious light appear on the night sky that was hovering above the lake.

Chapter 5: Tammy Stone

Tammy Stone (24) was traveling along a uninhabited road, on her way back home to Waco in Texas around the time of her birthday in 1973. The driver had just finished her evening shift at the diner which she was employed at and spent approximately fifteen minutes. The time must have been around 2am. It was a sudden occurrence. She claims to "feel weird, like you were in a state of mind or a dream." It was as if her ears felt strained and the sounds of her car was muffled. It was very alarming after a short time of becoming dizzy and lightheaded, with terrible vertigo, as well as a intense feeling of nausea.

It's hard to remember exactly what happened, but she was able to return at her place without incident but...it took a whopping 3 hours after. Over the following few nights, she was plagued with nightmares about the events and gradually was able to put the details of what transpired to her. And it wasn't a happy story.

The dream began with two tiny figures advancing at her car. The two figures caused the engine to stop, and the headlights to start flashing. They were five feet tall. As they opened the door of their car open, she realized that both were dressed with light blue, single-piece uniforms that had tight cap-styles. The sunken cheeks on their faces and their facial features appeared as thin. They did not communicate and they took her out of the car, and then carried her around her wrists and ankles into the spaceship.

She was positioned on a cold, hard area and had her clothes ripped off. The area was filled with 5 or 6 of these animals and a cold, metal device was inserted in her nose. Through the entire time she was being inspected, she noticed "a tiny machine which hung over me as if it had a huge eye and produced an eerie sound that made me feel sick" according to the words of her doctor. In what appeared to be just a couple of minutes, the machine was taken off her nostrils.

Then, she was dressed and carried back to her vehicle in the same painful manner and spooky way before being put in the driver's seat. They vanished, and, despite all the trauma, Tammy was able to start the vehicle again and make it back home.

The majority of abductees experience nightmares regarding what happened to them. However, they often require the assistance of professionals who are hypnotists that can help them recall certain events. Even though this was an extremely violent and scary incident, the girl could fill in the missing 3 hours of her day through putting the dreams of her future into her own.

The reality that Tammy was not subjected to an esoteric hypnosis treatment and her situation was not picked into consideration by the many passionate individuals or official organizations, is probably the reason for our having no information on what she did to get her life back in order following this incident.

Chapter 6: The Pascagoula Abduction
Charles Hickson And Calvin Parker

Despite their different ages, Charles Hickson (42) and Calvin Parker (19) were great friends and shared an interest in fishing that was shared. They decided to go on going fishing in the evening after work on the 11th of October, 1973. They all resided within Gautier within Mississippi and were about to settle on one of their favorite hot spots along the Pascagoula River, when they were able to hear a weird buzzing noise from behind.

When they turned around, they were astonished to find an enormous egg-shaped glowing object measuring 10 by 8 feet almost 30 feet away from the shore, and at least a few feet higher than the sea. The object was illuminated by a blueish-blue illumination on what appeared to be the entrance and the door was opened, releasing the most intensely brilliant glow. With the light on, they could see three humanoid figures floating through the waters in the direction of. The creatures did not look aggressive, however they appeared to be very strange and eerie looking. Around 5 feet tall, they had heads that were shaped like bullets and set right on their shoulders, and the skin was very wrinkled and grey. The mouths were slit-like and had none of their eyes were visible, though they could be hidden due to the wrinkles. The most bizarre part was that, the place one would expect to see ears and a nose the conical things hanging out of their head in an angle. Both Charles as well as Calvin have later stated that they thought it was like an iceberg stuck to the snowman's head! The feet were all rounded and, when they swung instead of walking, their legs could have merged to form one leg. Certainly, there were two large arms, with claw-like hands. They acted as if they were robots. However, their actions were swift. Two animals took Charles in his arms, and he was unable to be able to move or fight. He witnessed Calvin move "limp" when the third creature grabbed his body. Then Calvin claimed that he fallen unconscious from fear during this time. Both Charles as well as Calvin were "floated" across to the spaceship.

Charles claims he was taken to a bright and uninviting room, in which it was evident that he had been hanging. Eye-like objects, approximately as big as an average ball, slid off its wall from it and "hung suspended in mid-air, with no apparent connection to another component of the chamber" when it moved slowly through his body during a thorough exam. The eye then moved back towards the wall. Charles was unable to observe Calvin aboard the vessel, but Charles was alone for twenty minutes. Then he was brought back to the shore and there was Calvin lying on the ground in tears and pleading. He spotted the spaceship shooting upwards and dissolving fast.

After the group had come together enough to think about what they should do and what to do, they decided to call the local Kessler Air Base. Kessler advised them to contact their local sheriff. Which they did.

The way in which the information about the events got to the media was not did, however within a few hours the entire town was in outrage. A lot of investigations followed, which included each of the men taking part in, and passing the lie detector test. Charles experienced a form of hypnosis that was regressive however, this was removed when he was too terrified to carry on. The night affected both of their lives tremendously, but it was not as smooth as would be expected considering their distinct experiences.

Charles who was witness to the action in Korea Charles, who had seen action in Korea, was able understand what was happening and was interested in UFO sightings afterward. When he reflected, he wondered what if these creatures could have actually been just robots and controlled by someone further away. Two more encounters with aliens, he claims. One occurred in February 1974 while the holiday was in an area for tree-growing commercially. The same kind of craft, and says; "There was just a message to me from them that they didn't intend to do us harm". In May, while the family was returning after a trip to see relatives, another craft was spotted in a field close to the highway they were traveling along. Charles' family members did not require him to step out of his car, but Charles noticed familiar silhouettes of the windows of the craft.

Calvin however, on his part was more disturbed by what had transpired and even had an emotional breakdown a couple of years later. Perhaps the youth of his generation had caused him to hide things was difficult for him to share and that led to increased tensions within himself? It is backed up by the fact that almost twenty years later, He admitted that he'd never actually fainted at that time like he originally stated. He said that he'd was placed on a sloped table, and that an alien was actually injecting an ingredient into the bottom of the penis. He further stated that he was feeling an eerie sense of danger during the abduction.

Later, Calvin too claimed a second encounter with the first female alien that had examined Calvin. He claims that she been trying to convince her that she was a believer in the identical God like he did, and also that the Bible is a genuine source of information.

Chapter 7: Sergeant Charles L Moody

In the Holloman Airforce Base in Alamogordo, New Mexico and interested in astronomy Charles Moody drove into the desert on the 13th of August, 1975, in order to view the meteor shower that was expected. The thing he didn't expect to witness was the spacecraft of an alien!

He was awake at 1:15am and noticed a glowing disc that was speedily falling through the skies. It was massive approximately 50 feet in length and possibly between 18 and 20 feet in width. It was metallic in appearance. The object was unstable in its direction as it sank and moved about 20 feet off the ground before beginning to accelerate directly toward the man. He slid into his car, and could have fled however he was not able to begin the vehicle.

The object slowed down about 70 feet from the scene and Charles noticed the high-pitched humming noise. Charles could see something that looked like figures from the rectangular windows. It stopped suddenly and Charles began to feel his body go completely numb. He was shook to the core, tried his engine again, and this time it responded, and he raced off, while the car sprang up before disappearing.

After returning home, it was apparent that he did only account for a little over one and a half hour. After a few hours the pain was felt at the lower part of his back. in the following days, there was a bump that appeared throughout the body. Doctors were puzzled, and, when Charles informed him of"missing time "missing time", he gave Charles the technique of self-hypnosis for seeking out the reason for why he was suffering.

Charles gradually put the story into his own mind. He recalled that after the sound had stopped, two giants (6 feet) took him from the vehicle. Charles recalls a fierce resistance and then a fight ensued. The unconscious man was laid on a slab of a type, in the vessel. In a state of incapacity, he saw a taller man, however clearly an authority figure, who was speaking to him through virtual communication.

The captain asked Charles whether he'd like to end the resistance he was displaying to being captured and, when Charles was willing to agree then the leader slapped an iron rod to his back. This lifted his crippling condition. Sergeant Moody is not aware of having been examined in any manner and was considered a guest on the ship and toured around the ship. He was shown the technology that was powering the ship. The system said it was a long rod with three glass-covered openings running throughout the length. Within each dome of glass was a crystal like object, which was flanked by two rods that were smaller each with a rounded end, and the other with a T-shaped slant. Charles felt the sweet, almost overwhelming smell that hung over the vessel.

Other than the differences in height each of the creatures were the same in appearance.

Their heads appeared large and hairless. They also had a an elongated brow. They had slim lips with small ears, round eyes with greyish skin. The leader wore an all-white silver suit, but the rest of them were wearing the skin-tight black suits.

The commander said that they were on an aircraft that was landing and"the "Mother vessel" was waiting to see them return hundreds of miles from the Earth's surface. Also, he made the bizarre announcement that even though Charles will see them once more however, it could take twenty years until they returned to earth however he did not provide any justification to justify the announcement. The man then placed his hands over both sides of Charles his head. Charles fell unconscious and was relegated to his vehicle, and he was able to wake up.

Chapter 8: Travis Walton

Seven woodcutters worked hard trimming down the timber of the National Forest of Apache-Sitgreaves in Arizona. Travis Walton (22) was exhausted and happy that his shift was coming to an close. The time was around 6pm on the 5th of November, 1975. The group of men got into the vehicle of the crew, and headed to home via the trail that was bull-dozed. The men all noticed an orange glow in the woods and as the path swung to their right, they could see "a bright object with a shape like a round disc" that was hovering around 20 feet over a clearing. Everyone saw it, in the same spot. Mike Rogers, the driver and head of the company took the truck off of the road.

Travis was extremely excited and leapt out of the way, advancing fast towards the object with the slightest fear. While he was moving towards the object the object, he heard a mix of a sound that sounded like an eerie sound. It appeared as though the object changed direction. In a moment of fear, he stopped and, to those onlookers, the flash of green and blue sprang out from beneath the vessel, giving Travis with a massive blow to the middle of his chest. The flash appeared to be an high-voltage electrical shock which raised him from the ground, sending his body outstretched around 20 feet to the woods. The terrified and brave passengers drove off in their vehicle and stood at the safe far distance as a glowing illumination appeared to rise up from the region and then disappear into the north-east, in the dark sky.

The group retreated to the scene, but they couldn't find any proof of what had occurred - nor did they track down Travis. They made a quick getaway to their nearest city, Heber and informed the Sheriff. Believing that it was a hoax, and not wanting to appear negligent, Sheriff Perkins took the search team returning to the spot which came up with nothing.

Five days after the incident, Travis found himself in darkness in the dark, lying in a stomach position on an icy road in Herber. He was starving, weak, thirsty and saw an unidentified UFO vanish when he was able to regain consciousness. He was quite in pain but was able reach an 'phone.

Travis phoned his sister. when the family came to pick him up and he was shocked to realize he'd been away for five days. Travis was able to be able to account for a short portion of the time and it was not an enjoyable story.

Travis remembers waking up at the floor with an oval-shaped device in his chest. There were tiny, silent appearing creatures sporting huge, glowing, brown eyes that dominated huge, unbald heads. They had none of their eyebrows, eyelashes or eyelashes. They had tiny, delicate hands and were dressed in the same color seamless suede suits. He swiftly pushed the equipment off and scoured the room in search of a weapon to use to defend himself after he fell off the table. Surprised, the beasts left the space.

Travis was on the lookout for an escape route when he was surprised to see the taller man advancing towards the way. He was dressed in blue a jumpsuit as well as an unmarked helmet. He said that Travis must go with his direction. Travis attempted to talk to the person who did not speak to him however, he led him into an area that was smaller. He was able to find three people and a woman, but they did not, either. to the other. They forced him to the table, and he became in the presence of what appeared appear to be a tiny oxygen mask that was strapped to a black sphere that was the size of the size of a golf ball. The man doesn't recall anything else, before waking up in Herber.

It remains to be one of the best-documented and controversial instances of abductions by aliens on record.

Chapter 9: The Stanford Abductions

Louise Smith (44) and Elaine Thomas (48)

Mona, Louise and Elaine were able to decide on a spur-of the moment outing for dinner in celebration of Mona's birthday and Louise's brand-new automobile. It was quite late when they started out...about 8:15, on the 6th of January 1976. The three of them lived within Liberty, Kentucky, but went for lunch at The Redwood Restaurant near Lancaster. All of them were interested in the arts and Louise would like to sketch the painting she saw being displayed inside the restaurant. After a relaxing, but non-alcoholic evening they headed home along Highway 78 at about 11pm at night, when they were aware of a massive glowing red-colored object descending upon their vehicle. The initial thought was an airplane in trouble but when it came closer towards them, they realized it was actually a disc-shaped metallic with an elongated dome, and highlighted by the red light strip at the center, and a the flashing yellow light coming at the base of the object.

Louise driver she was scared to see the vehicle accelerate when the object fell in front of the Chevy. While she stepped away from the pedal, it started increasing its speed and she realized she was no longer in control over the car. The interior of the car was bright with a bluish flash, followed by a blurred "sort like fog" and the three women were stung by a burning sensation which forced them to close their eyes. The three of them had a sense of their car being "backed up" in between "old stones" to either side. And then, all of a sudden they were to the road and were returning home as normal!

When they returned home safe however, they realised that they'd "lost" some time. Everyone was extremely nervous and found burn spots on their necks, as well as the other areas of flesh that were exposed. Louise was especially upset that her pet bird did not provide her with his typical happy salutation and in actual appeared to be scared of her.

Over the next few months, women all shed considerable weight, and the guilt of what happened rested over them all. Everyone were aware that an entire time and half had gone not recorded the night they were all believed that it was the incident that occurred during the same time and that had an adverse effect in their daily lives.

Then, they began regression hypnosis. This proved that each of them had been through an entirely different, but incredibly horrific encounter. All of them had been brutally scrutinized physically and held in humiliating and embarrassing places, even though there was no sexual assaults as such. Louise recalls being placed on a desk and scrutinized by creatures that had hands that looked like wing tips with jagged edges. Mona recalls being put in a slumbering position some type of chair. Elaine experienced very painful memories of being trapped in an "capsule" which had an "hose-like" tie in her neck that was tightened each time she attempted to talk. Elaine also spoke of an instrument that resembled a tube, with a curly end, which was used to poke her chest. Everybody remembered having a warming liquid sprayed on their bodies and faces, and having eyes that appeared to be hovering over their bodies. They communicated with the aliens in a very limited way and communicated only via telepathic communication. They were seen by all women as extremely spooky characters, approximately four feet tall, who were floating around quietly.

The incident clearly resulted in a media storm that didn't help the group members cope with what occurred to them. The group all passed the "lie detection" test with ease and, for the rest of their lives, their lives were shattered through flashbacks and the aftermath of their horrific experience.

Chapter 10: The Allargash Abductions
Jack And Jim Weiner (Twins)

Charlie Foltz and Chuck Rak (Tour guide)

The group of college friends who were all in their 20's they were taking part in an 11-day trip through the Allargash Wilderness Waterways in Maine. The second night, they spotted a large light in the sky. When they were able to decide which light it was the object seemed to collapse and then disappear. A few days later, on the 26th of August, 1976, they established their camp at Lake Eagle and decided on an evening fishing trip. They decided to take the risk to build a huge campfire, stocked with to fuel the fire for several hours to lead them back to campsite, and then depart with the canoe...with the idea of trout. After a few minutes, they spotted that same glowing light that was visible in the sky above the trees. The second time it was different, however the sky was able to vibrate with different hues of red, green as well as off-white and yellow with a spinning display of apparent energy.

To test the absurdity of it Charlie utilized a flashlight indicate the SOS and the vessel quickly began to move toward them. It was a shock and they began rowing toward the bank, in a state of panic. They saw a flash of light and an oval beam of light flew over the waters and completely embraced them as well as the boat. Within a few seconds they were sitting on the bank and viewing the spacecraft when it appeared to explode at the edge of the water before reappearing in the skies. The ashes of the enormous burning fire that they created indicated that at most 2 to 3 hours had passed with none of being aware of what happened. Everyone was exhausted and depleted of energy and simply retreated the stairs to their sleeping mattresses.

The incidents of that night never were thought of, though members of the group suffered from periodic dreams, especially Jack who developed an obsession with maths and Physics. The situation changed when Jim suffered a serious head accident 12 years later and his nightmares got more frequent.

The nightly dreams were of strange beings with necks that were long, doing damage that affected his genitals as his body was paralyzed or swaying in mattress. The year was 1988. Jim shared his experience before a group of people at an UFO gathering and a probe, that included all four of the men, began.

They all experienced regressive hypnosis and they all shared the same account of being awakened aboard the spaceship which one of them said was "looking as a veterinary office". The men were all told via telepathy that if they cooperated with each other, they could not suffer harm. Four men went through identical procedures and observed each other as they were assessed. The men were instructed to remove their clothes and a torch-like instrument was utilized to examine the eyes and mouths of their patients. While they sat in a circle to lay on tables various hand-held instruments were utilized to examine their faces closely. They were also asked to take specimens from saliva, skin scrapings urine, faeces, and Sperm.

The two were tied to a harness as well as their legs and arms were stretched. The whole time they felt completely helpless like an external force was exerting control of their minds over the people. Then they were told to put on their clothes and were taken to a different room that had an entrance to one side. The strange feeling, which they couldn't describe was felt as they were manipulated by a man through the portal. They floated to the bottom before being re-emerged in the canoe.

Since the group of friends completed their studies in art at the college level and were able draw a variety of sketches of their impressions of their abductor. They are mostly humanoid characters with huge shiny, glowing eyes that have no lids. They also sport fingers that are four fingers like insect.

Chapter 11: Dechmont Forest Abduction

Robert Taylor (61) was an experienced forester who lived near Livingstone, West Lothian in Scotland. On November 9, 1979, he left his home in his pickup together with his red setter Lara in order to inspect his young trees that he put in the previous day. It was 10:15 am when he pulled up alongside the M8 motorway, and drove on the Dechmont trail. When he came to a turn on the track, the trail, he encountered the shape of a "spaceship".

It was round and about 20 feet wide it was 12 feet tall and hovering quietly, just a few feet over the ground. It was flat and had a thin, shelf-like rim that ran about its circumference, and stems that were topped by propellers that were placed regularly. Its primary colour was dark grey. But it had translucent highlights, and Robert could feel the trees that were on the opposite side of the structure. The color was unstable and Robert stated that it looked an attempt to "camouflage" itself. Two mini spheres fell off the ground and moved toward him with a ferocious speed. Each was around 3 feet wide, with the spikes protruding outwards, which produced the "plopping" sound when they were rolled across the floor. Robert was not too shocked to get scared and that they resembled Navy mines that were used during that time of the Second World War. The smell was acrid that smelt like brake linings flaming out. This made him be breathless. Then he lost consciousness when the balls bonded themselves to his clothes and felt like he was getting dragged toward the bigger ball.

The moment he arrived the corner, there was nothing odd on the horizon; it was all he saw was a screeching, engaged dog running around about him. The man was shocked to discover that he'd lost his voice and was not able communicate with the dog. Also, he was suffering from headaches but was unable to stand up on his feet, and was very thirsty. He began to walk up the track in the best way possible, but after some time could move with his legs even though the feeling of being sick was extremely strong.

The driver did not have enough vocal capability to operate the two-way radio until it was time to pick up the truck. The car wouldn't begin and, having no option, Robert had to walk to home for a mile. The wife of his, Mary told him that he looked like a pity after he arrived home approximately 11:15am. However, in the end it was possible to make a sound that was strong enough to claim that he had received a beating... with "a Spaceship!"

The doctor was contacted and noticed a bruise under his chin, and an worse graze that was more severe in his left leg however, he deemed him to be healthy. The pants, however, were ripped to pieces in both legs. After Robert created an outline of the sequence of incident with the police they calculated that he might be in a state of unconsciousness for up to 20 minutes. Did he get abducted? In contrast to others who were abducted, Robert never developed subsequent mental or physical health issues. Robert never experienced nightmares, or thoughts of alien creatures. He died in 2007 at age of 88.

The site did have physical evidence that backed his claim. The officers who were assessing the location and found a circular spot in which the grass was smoothed out, however there were no marks. "Something circular" was emitting energy and could have floated, but it hasn't dropped on the spot. There were two set of track markings that looked like ladders around 2.5 meters long, which cannot be explained by anyone and 40 distinct marks on the earth...little hole that appeared that they were created through spikes of a certain kind.

Livingstone is situated in what's named "Falkirk Triangle" The area is home to at least 300 accounts of UFO sightings per year.

Chapter 12: Whitley Strieber

Whitley Strieber was a wildly famous fiction writer who wrote about supernatural and horror stories that included out-of-body experiences after he experienced an experience with himself, that according to his own words "completely altered my perception of reality by reversing each and every certainty I believed in."

The man was away on vacation, with his son and wife at a remote house located in Upper State New York. It was just after 11pm on the 23rd of December, 1985 and everyone had gone home to bed having carefully set the modern alarm system that was just recently put in place. Whitley was awakened a few hours after to discover a bizarre appearance humanoid in his bedroom. The next minute there was a solitary spot in the woods just outside of the house, with no idea of how he came there.

It is one thing, but seeing it happen was quite another. Especially in the case of a bizarre scratch on the side of your head, which was a sign of something awry. Whitely approached a well-known UFO researcher, and went through many sessions of regressive hypnosis to understand the events that transpired to the man. He slowly regained his memory and he could recall the moment he woke awake, even though he initially saw only one tiny, mechanical creature but there were numerous of them. They "floated" the man from the bed into an unidentified UFO waiting to be seen.

Whitley was subjected tests for medical purposes, including the injection of a long needle through his brain, and the usage of an electrode that was inserted in the rectum of his body to collect the semen sample and the draw of blood from his fingers. When he was hypnotized, Whitley was able to discern four distinct kinds of aliens he met during the evening. There was the "robot" kind that was present in his bedroom, the same, bulky kind which were not robots A slimmer, more tall "weak-looking" kind with huge eyes that slant upwards and others with a similar physical structure, however with eyes that were black similar to buttons.

As bizarre as it was, ongoing hypnosis showed that this was not by any by any means the only encounter with aliens during Whitley's lifetime. Whitley had actually met with numerous people, beginning during his early years. Through time it became possible to recollect several experiences in detail, and discovered that he'd traveled through time as well as space, with the people he calls "visitors". When he was 13 the inventor had constructed the "anti-gravity" machine, and had frequently was able to hear voices from other realms via his hi-fi system. Following the event on Christmas Eve the man was diagnosed being suffering from Temporal Lobe Epilepsy that is an condition that can cause hallucinations. Whitley has completely refuted the diagnosis in light of the lessons he gained from his regressive hypnosis sessions. Whitley started a support group with others

Alien abductees. He also runs the website "Unknown country".

Following the events of 1985, He wrote three books on the events of 1985, which are among the top bestsellers: Communion in 1987, Transformation in 1988; and Confirmation of!998. On his site on August 5, 2007 he wrote an article titled "What did my semen go through?"

He describes what happened to him back in 1985 to "rape" and claims that in 1988, he saw a beautiful, gorgeous baby by a group of "visitors" who he met at the bottom of the Upstate home he was leasing. There was a feeling that the baby had some connection to him, and has been experiencing an uneasy, numb sensation of sadness since the day.

Chapter 13: Abduction On The North Canol Road

Kevin resided in Ross River in the Yukon in Canada. Kevin decided to take a break to hunt moose and, after loading his equipment onto his motorbike to ride up his North Canol Road. He reached what was to serve as his base of operations in a trailer located at Dewhurst Creek, a little earlier than nightfall on September 2, 1987.

The following morning, the next day, he departed early and bright, headed toward Macpass which is a moose habitat. The moose spotted him stopping for a bathroom break and to take in the views in this beautiful and untouched area and was stunned to see initially what appeared to be an aeroplane possibly an DC3 and a blizzard at a distance of just 500 yards from. While he viewed it move slow between north and south around 40 meters above surface, he recognized that it wasn't a typical aircraft. It had a cigar-shaped shape, dark green with portsholes that ran in gray strips around its edges, to the extent that it was visible. Two other strange aspects of this craft It was silent. There was no sound whatsoever and the craft appeared to "partially disappear and come back to its original forme" while Kevin observed. The craft moved in the direction of the shape of a cone and didn't reappear at the other end.

Unnerved, Kevin was pleased to hear the sound of a metallic clang that sounded like an open trunk being closed on an automobile, fading away from view ahead of the car. Kevin hurried along the road before he came around the corner looking for a person who may have seen similar sights. The two aliens around 20 feet from him. Kevin recalls thinking they didn't look anything like the typical "little green guys" which are frequently smacked about. They were five feet tall, dressed in the light blue of one-piece jumpsuits. They had large heads, large eyes, sharp faces and appeared more like insect-like creatures more than anything else. The legs and arms were easily identifiable as insects however, they were very thin. One of them raised his hand, and then there was an illuminating flash around the waist and Kevin went black.

After he had a moment to think when he woke up, he was in the opposite direction of the road. There was nothing visible other than his bicycle, which was in the wrong direction that road. Astonished, Kevin headed back to the trailer. When he finally got there that the entire time had passed by. While he was making coffee to settle his nerves, the next thing he noticed was the sound of a deep, booming hum coming from outside. There was also a slight sound that filled the trailer. The sound lasted for 10 minutes before Kevin thought he couldn't take the outside view which is why he fell asleep.

He was able to sleep well and at night, began experiencing flashbacks of the events that took place during the day. These memories weren't in a continuous fashion, but were more like sequential images. Following being "shot" in the light source, Kevin recalls feeling like stretching out and speeding upwards at a high speed, with massive areas of landscape passing beneath his feet. He then lay on the bed in complete darkness. At that point, it appeared like the dark "peeled from the bed" and he could see at the eyes of an grey-colored creature more akin to humans than the eyes that he'd seen in the dirt. There was a voice inside his head that was telling him that there wasn't anything to worry about. He recalls actually inquiring of the alien, who was very welcoming to know if they intended to conduct experiments on him. Kevin heard in his mind, the creature claim that it was already completed the experiment. Aside from the odd sensation on his hands, Kevin didn't feel anything uncomfortable, nor did he be afraid.

Grey asked Kevin if it would be possible to observe his planet, and after Kevin answered "Yes" the gray led him to a porthole, and revealed a brilliant white star. Kevin's astronomy skills were not enough to tell if this was real or it was not. Kevin noticed a big device with buttons at the top that looked similar to the copier right in front of the glass, and the grey demanded that he not get close to the machine. The grey asked whether he wanted to travel and Kevin answered "No no, I'm not ready at this point". There were greys on the ship however he only interacted with grey. He was then given the glass with a yellow color that he wanted Kevin to drink, so to forget the incident. Kevin stated that he did not wish to erase the incident and his abductor/friend suggested that it was better for him if he remembered. Kevin clearly remembers placing the glass back down after three sips, and wasn't forced to finish the drink.

Kevin didn't speak about any of these incidents to the two people who later joined him for the last portion of his vacation. In the few weeks after the incident when Kevin discovered the habit of often rubbing his hands. Kevin was shocked to discover after examining them, that there were distinctive "scoop marks" across each hand. It is likely that the markings were the result of something which occurred at the time of abduction. However, Kevin is not able to recall exactly what transpired during the "examination" the only minor discomfort that he can recall, has an unpleasant burning sensation that he felt in his hands. It is quite rare for there to be physical evidence of alien abduction and the account that Kevin eventually wrote of his experience and it is available, with many illustrations at: http://www.ufobc.ca/yukon/n-canol-abd/index.htm#investigation. This is a compelling tale.

Chapter 14: Ilkley Moor Alien The Philip Spenser Abduction

NB. The case can be mistaken for the case from Alan Godfrey in 1980.

Ilkely Moor is a mysterious region of the countryside that is mostly comprised of peat bogs that lie at 1,319 feet higher than sea-level within West Yorkshire in the United Kingdom. It has the appearance of an old-fashioned land packed with prehistoric cairn stones protecting ancient tales. In the glare of day. It is generally wind-swept, isolated and surrounded by fogs, low clouds and fogs. The area is believed to be plagued by mysterious creatures as well as the swaying, hovering lighting. Folks from the earth have explained the strange phenomena because there are two runways near by: Leeds Bradfort Airport and Menwith Hill Military Base. Menwith Hill Military Base. The events that occurred prior to sundown 1 December 1987 can't be explained in this way.

Philip Spenser, an ex London policeman who had recently relocated to the Moors along with his wife and son to be nearer to their family. He left at around 7:15am, equipped with a GPS, because his new surroundings were not acquainted with the landscape as well as his camera. The plan was to stroll across the moors and to get to the house of his father-in-law and capture some great shots of the intriguing and bizarre designs and lighting patterns which are typical for the area. The camera was loaded with the appropriate ASH rating film.

In the process of obtaining just the right angles, he saw a figure appear in the camera and instantly clicked the shutter. When he looked upwards and saw the silhouette, he noticed an intense humming sound. was able to see the gesturing to him to move away, and then speed off and sway before disappearing over an outcrop on the road. Philip was chasing him, and when he came to a halt almost ran into the shape of a saucer made of metallic featuring a domed roof, which was topped by a light-colored rectangular. The craft sprang up rapidly and disappeared into the fog with incredible speed.

A bit confused, Philip decided to walk into the village nearest to him. In trying to utilize his compass, and he noticed that it was polarized. had been reversed. As it was time to enter the village thirty moments later, the he found that he'd had lost two hours of his morning.

After the film was processed, he was ecstatic to find that there was indeed an undistinct, but, nevertheless, an undeniable picture of what he'd observed. This was then the first image taken by a photographer that was of an alien, and it obviously, it triggered an avalanche of test results from any interested body. The image was deemed authentic, unaltered by any means, and absolutely no species on the planet.

Philip finally gave in to the inevitable regressive hypnosis in order to recall his memories of his lost time. Philip discovered that he had indeed been lifted in the aircraft just before it took off. Though he had been scrutinized closely and even a thorough examination through the "illuminating device" A voice promised him that he'd not suffer any harm and there was no reason to be worried.

The abductors he was talking to were described as short and with big black eyes, huge eyes, small lips and no noses. Arms were lengthy, culminating in hands that had only three fingers. The shuffled gait is due to the fact that both legs came to a V shape. feet that had a look of two toes per foot. On board, they watched two different series of images or films. One of them was a bleak account of the ecological damage humankind has caused to Earth to date. He did not want to reveal the contents of the other movie - only stating that he'd committed to keeping the film secret.

When hypnotized and recalling the event, he viewed through some of the windows. an account of the tape reads:

"Oh! God! (sounds stunned) Are you sure? (deep breath) (pause) (sounds scared) ...don't wish to be here. Do you want to go down? I hear the voice saying that you're got no reason to be afraid. I didn't know it was that beautiful."

Following the Regressive therapy, Philip realized that he took the photo when he had left the facility as his guest was waved goodbye to him.

Chapter 15: The Father And Son Were Abducted By The Police

John Salter Jr. (55) as well as John Salter, his brother John (23) drove to the conference at New Orleans, Mississippi where John Jr. was scheduled to give a speech about "Civil Rights and Self Defense". The sun was setting on the 20th of March, 1988. It was around 6:25 when they approached a stretch of four-lanes along Highway 14. When 7:45 came around the group was traveling in the opposite direction of the direction they ought to have gone and had no clue what had brought the reverse from, or what transpired to the 1 hour 20 minutes. The two drove towards Bettendorf in the evening, where they stayed for the evening. In the morning they headed towards the east. Around 10:14am with the sun shining brightly the two of them became conscious of a bright silver sparkling light moving towards them along the highway. When it came closer and became more massive, they saw the shape of a saucer with the dome tilted as if in greeting while it was soaring above the cabin of the truck and then disappeared in the sky.

Three months later when John Jr. started having glimpses of dreams which allowed his son and him to complete the details of the events that took place during the late evening of the night. They were "forced" away from the main road and onto a treacherous and narrow road, which was where they parked their pickup. They were standing in front of the cabin as six or 7 tiny humanoids emerged and made their way up the back of the bumpers to inspect their equipment. They sat approximately 4 feet tall and thin with relatively large heads and eyes that slant. A sudden taller form was seen arriving. It was remarkably like a person who is 6 feet tall dressed in non-descript, but well clothing. The aliens communicated telepathically, gently to John Jr. and his son must follow as they walked through dark woods as they walked along the ravine finally, up over a tiny hill. One time, John Jr stumbled and immediately many aliens came to the side of him to help keep the man on his path.

The second memory is of an extremely brightly lit space which had a blue shining panel to one side. The patients were seated in the shape of dental chairs. While they had been "immobilized" and were not offered an option however, the exam that ensued was performed carefully and cautiously. The object was placed deep into John Jr.'s left nostril. He received injections in his neck and upper chest. His son was watching as his facial features were scanned by a torch-like instrument that had the most unusual, soft, malleable head that was melted to the shape of bone structures.

Then they appeared outside and the taller man was there to accompany them back to the pickup and they left in a profound feeling of sadness and loss. The unspoken agreement was that they would see each other in the future, even though this never been the case.

Chapter 16: The Linda Cortile-Napolitano Abduction

Sometimes, it is referred to Manhattan. Manhattan

Abduction or the Brooklyn Bridge Abduction.

Linda Cortile (41) had just fallen asleep at around 3 am on the 30th of November 1989. After waking up, she noticed an numbness that was paralyzing and then became conscious of numerous "grey creature" within her 12th floor apartment. They swept her off of mattress and into the window. When she was outside, she stepped up in the air and was dragged up by the beam of light into a spacecraft that was hovering. In the spacecraft it was a long hallway that led her through a corridor lined with regular benches, and then through a series of sliding doors to a well-lit room. The woman was conscious of various buttons, but the space was mostly dominated by a huge table. When she was lowered to the table it was possible for her to start screaming, however there was a person who "greys" put his hands on her mouth and said something that sounded similar to "Nobbyegg" in her. The woman is aware that she was questioned, but is unable to recall specific particulars. What she can recall is that she was thrown back to her bed, with her husband whom she had slept with for the whole abduction.

It turned out that Linda was in contact with UFO specialist Budd Hopkins after having read the book. Linda initially approached him after she had an enigmatic memory of being abducted thirteen years ago and believed that it was something related to an area of bump she observed close to her nose. After meeting Hopkins Linda, she enrolled in the support group for abductees.

Then, of course, she called Hopkins to inform him of this latest development. She agreed to use hypnosis with regressive effects to attempt to clarify the details of what transpired on November 30. An routine scan showed a tiny oval-shaped metallic object within her nose. A few weeks later, Linda had a severe nosebleed. The next morning, it was discovered that the item vanished. It's unclear what the purpose of this object was. It is unclear if it was implanted in the course of her first or the second abduction. It is likely to be the first abduction since there was evidence of cartilage that had accumulated, which indicated that something which was there for a long time and was taken away.

In 1991, Hopkins received two correspondences from people who claimed that they had witnessed Linda's abduction. The incident exploded to the forefront of news since it was the first case of abduction that had eyeswitnesses who are independent. "Dan" as well as "Richard" reached out to Hopkins and claimed to be worried and concerned about the girl who they witnessed being kidnapped. They stated that it's been bothering them for several months and had a devastating affect on their lives. it was the reason why they finally decided to take action to stop the situation. They explained that they were bodyguards who had been escorting an individual who was visiting an airport in the area when their car was came to a stop. They stepped up to move the vehicle and marvelled as the woman, dressed in the white dress with her hair curled into an emaciated position, floats through the window of an apartment with a group of men sporting large heads but little hair. The entire group had swam into an enormous oval floating craft, which was hovering and then vanished.

The third letter came sent by a woman whose name was her self Janet Kindle. She claimed she was walking on the Brooklyn Bridge a little after 3 am on November 30 the 30th, and her vehicle as well as other vehicles around her were all stuck. She recalled seeing four figures, all in a in a fetal position floating out from a window, and then being pulled into the brightest of craft. She claimed that the lights were too bright for her to have blind her eyes in order to be able to see the motions.

The more Hopkins investigated the incident, the more difficult it became. "Dan" as well as "Richard" were initially claiming to be bodyguards, later claimed to be police officers. However, after Hopkins received a second email from a third-party it was discovered that they were actually CIA agents who were who were assigned to none other then Javier Perez de Cuellar, Secretary of the United Nations. The Secretary was also witness to the kidnapping, but was not willing to release a an explanation at the time. After the CIA became involved, the speculations and rumours became difficult to discern from factual information. Linda was caught between the two of the CIA, was kidnapped by a variety of federal agencies two times before she began to feel like she was an alien in her own right, specifically because of her initial abduction.

Bud Hopkins published his book on the topic titled "Witnessed" in the year 1996. While the abduction caused a lot of excitement and publicity but it was not able to provide any useful data to the corpus of research which is the basis of our understanding of the extraterrestrial presence on our planet.

Chapter 17: Kelly Cahill

Kelly Cahill (27), her husband Andrew along with their three children were traveling across the Dandenong Foothills, near Belgrave, Victoria in Australia on the 8th of August, 1993. They were driving to celebrate a birthday at 7 pm at the time Kelly saw an orange light that was quite low in the air and hovering above a field. Andrew dismissed it as something else and then they didn't think about the sight.

After celebrating their birthdays, they began their homeward journey shortly prior to midnight. In the exact same location when they returned when they saw the bright glowing orange light once more. This time, Andrew did not look at it with awe because, as they sat there the light, they could observe that the light was caused by lighting coming out of the windows that were arranged over a vessel or something similar to it. Kelly believed she could glimpse human silhouettes appearing in the windows. The craft suddenly veered to the left, then disappeared. Just 2 kilometers later, a blinding, intense white illumination appeared just ahead of the vehicle. Andrew thought it was far too late to make any alternative other than driving straight across it. Then, suddenly it was all normal and they continued to drive in a relaxed 40 miles an hour.

The two returned home in good spirits, but the two of them smelt of vomit from the vehicle and Kelly believed that they'd somehow missed more time as 1 1/2 hours during the drive to home. The husband of the couple thought they were just reminiscing about the time they gone to see their buddies. They both did not feel well. Both were experiencing stomachaches that night. Kelly specifically, seemed extremely tired and irritable. She was also shocked to discover a bizarre triangle-shaped mark below her navel while she was removing her clothes. The woman also had unannounced menstrual blood that evening and later developed an Uterine infection, which needed hospitalization within a few weeks.

While Kelly was disturbed by her dreams at night, the bizarre incident was almost forgotten until Andrew mentions them during the barbeque just a few days afterwards. It was clear that this had triggered Kelly's memory, and she began to recall vivid, non-sequenced however, very terrifying fragments of the events that had occurred and what proved to be a the absence of time. Even though she was not experiencing the regressive hypnosis until a few several years after, Kelly was able to connect the dots over the following weeks and what makes this particular case special is the fact that there were multiple people who were witnesses to the incident.

It is vital to know that Kelly was an Pentecostal fundamentalist who was primarily focused in enhancing her spiritual understanding. Andrew however, on contrary, was an orthodox Moslem and had great respect of his wife's desire towards a deeper connection with God.

After driving through the white, bright illumination, they had taken their car off the road and then walked out. They spotted an enormous spacecraft, which was at least 150 feet wide that landed on an open paddock on the other side of the road. When they were attempting to cross the road in its direction the other vehicle had stopped 150 yards farther along the road.

Three others (Bill, Jane and Glenda) were able to get out of the car behind them as well, and had also crossed the field in the direction of the lighting. The three of them saw a number of dark figures of black, at most seven feet tall, floating across the ground toward the light. They appeared to be completely uninteresting aside from massive, round, bright red eyes. Kelly was possessed of an the evil force and shouted in a panic that they were soulless beings. (Kelly was eventually psychotherapy and was recorded documented as saying these creatures are "arrogant as well as proud'. They they appeared to "be filled with hatred of humans" and made fun of her faith that in God.) The aliens were divided into two groups; one group was headed toward Kelly as well as her family, while the second group was directed towards the three persons that were taken from the second vehicle. The humans who were involved all have very sporadic memories of being inspected in extremely painful and embarrassing manners. There are memories of beasts of black stepping on their bodies naked - and even "kissing" the navels. Every woman were covered in the same triangular mark on their navels. Glenda suffered from ligature scars at the ankle of one, like she was held by force.

Bill, Jan and Glenda reported that there may have an additional vehicle that stopped and was further away from the hill. The trio could spot a man inside the vehicle, but no one witnessed him getting out, and hasn't been found as of yet. Some of them remember that the vehicle's lights were on, therefore, perhaps he drove with the fear of being caught?

The police investigating the incident made sure to keep the people in the two vehicles apart until they could give detailed descriptions of the events they remembered. All of them sketched the aliens and craft to the best of their ability. Each of the narratives and the drawings revealed amazing similarities. There was no doubt that the two people whom were completely unrelated to each other, had experienced an experience similar to the one that occurred on the night in August...there must be absolutely no doubt about that.

Chapter 18: An Alien Abduction Of A Family In Wales

The Great Orme is a mountain range which culminate in an emerald headland of limestone located in Llandudno, North Wales. It's a bizarre and enigmatic stretch of land as well as Llandudno is home to the site of a Neolithic burial site. It is a paved avenue with antiquated stones, called Hyglfa's Leirw that ends with the large, oblong enclosure of Liety Fadag. There are traces of round huts as well as stone circles dating from posts Roman and Medieval times are found...and this is the third likely spot on earth, where there is a chance to see UFOs!

The sightings of hundreds are recorded in and around Great Orme every year. One family, which remains unknown, witnessed more than just a glimpse on the 10th of November, 1997. A 92-year-old man living at Little Orme in Conwy was uneasy after observing a number of "frightening shining lights" in the words he used to describe as they swarmed across the mountainside for a number of consecutive nights immediately prior to the 10th November. The night of the incident when the family drove back home on the motorway Bodfair/Landernog as they noticed an immense triangular purple-colored craft that was pacing with their vehicle. With no warning, their whole vehicle was completely engulfed by the object. In the blink of an eye the next thing they knew, they were traveling along the highway in a normal manner... but the fact that it happened several hours after that.

That same evening, along the same street the businessman who was returning from a business meeting indeed stopped his vehicle in amazement, to examine the huge structure, which was about as big as the size of a football field. The thing was like "a spinner for a child." The man claims that it was surrounded with "a number of bright windows" and then he sketched an outline of the. He observed it hovering over houses in the city of Llandernog. He stated that he thought the size was sufficient to carry hundreds of people at the at the same time.

There isn't much information about the family that was in the vehicle which experienced the experience of a lifetime, other than that the person who was involved suffered teeth issues shortly after the incident and sought out a dentist to treat an issue with his upper molar. When he was at the dentist, the dentist noticed a dark object falling from the mouth of. The object was not determined and the man was forced to file a report about the night's bizarre incidents to local authorities.

After this, the family was visited by two simple-clothed men who claimed to be representatives of The Air Force. The family was told not to talk about the incident, nor reveal the incident publicly. Family members wanted to speak with someone about what had happened and finally shared the story with a friend who shared the story with a acquaintance. Another friend happens to have a connection with Margaret Fey and that was an opportunity to be lucky.

Margaret Fey has investigated the UFO phenomenon for more than 40 years. In 1993 she established her own organization, the "Welsh Fellowship of Ufologists Independent" in order to "turn novices into experienced experts in UFO research". She consulted and interviewed families who had been traumatized, but upon their request, kept their privacy. Fey nonetheless has the authority and credibility in this particular case that it should at the very least be included among the cases that merit serious attention regardless of the fact that we may never be able to know the full story...

Chapter 19: How Ufos Came To Be Or Might Be

UFOs also known as Unidentified Flying Objects (also referred to as unidentified air phenomena in plural (UAPs) are for a long time fascinated people across the world over a period of time. Examining their intentions, origins as well as their true nature is a source of heated debates and speculations among scientists as well as administrative authorities, scheme experts, and UFO fans. This article examine the multitude of theories that could explain the aspects of these perplexing UFOs, but refrain from looking into the validity of these statements.

The US government has always been cautious on UFOs and has often dismissed sightings as false identifications of natural phenomena, or human-made objects. In recent times authorities from the US Department of Defense has published videos and other information about interactions between pilots of military aircraft and unknown aerial phenomena (UAP) which is a name that is more popular than UFOs. Though the federal government has not provided definitive reasons for these incidents however, they have admitted the need for further research into UAPs and have rekindled interest in the topic.

A lot of scientists and researchers view UFOs with suspicion, usually pointing UFO sightings due to misidentifications of natural phenomena like meteors, weather balloons and even aircrafts that are conventional.

There are some scientists who suggest psychological theories, which suggest that individuals may interpret unclear signals as UFOs because of existing beliefs or assumptions. The scientific community usually requires extraordinary proof for exceptional claims, a few researchers are open to the possibility of alien life and are willing to think about alternative explanations to UFO-related sightings that can't be quickly discounted.

The UFO-loving and awe-inspiring provide a variety of explanations regarding UFO sightings. They range from aliens to extraterrestrial beings. There are those who believe UFOs are proof of advanced technology developed by other cultures, and are on Earth to fulfill various purposes, like scientific research extracting resources, for example, as well as monitoring human activity. Some speculate that UFOs could be humans who have traveled through time from the future, or even secret government initiatives like research aircraft or surveillance technologies.

The majority of UFO conspiracy theories involve government agencies and other powerful organizations concealing the truth about aliens through elaborate cover-ups. This suggests that the most powerful are aware of a great deal about the mysterious flying objects and might be able communicate with these aliens.

Certain conspiracy theorists believe the government has retrieved crashed UFOs as well as reverse engineered the technologies to use for military or other purposes. Others suggest that particular UFO sightings may be the result of psyops, or psychological operations, which aim to manipulate public perceptions or testing the effectiveness of new technology.

There isn't a decision on what exactly UFOs are.

The perspectives range from natural phenomena, misidentifications and misinformation to alien life on Earth and intricate conspiracies, the issue of UFOs remains a fascination and enthral people around the world. The understanding we have of UFOs will surely change with the new information and evidence that come to light.

It is important to approach this issue with an open and honest eye to differentiate the real from the fiction, and to understand the bizarre occurrences.

Investigation of Alien Existence - Delving deep into Drake Equation and Fermi Paradox

It's logical to think about whether there is intelligent life that exists beyond Earth in the vastness of the cosmic sphere and the countless galaxies and stars as well as planets.

When we consider that there are far more stars than sand grains on Earth and that a lot of them have planets, one can see the vastness of the universe. But, it is not foolish to think that we're the sole planet capable of sustaining life in the universe.

However, in this chapter we'll explore this subject with the help of the tools of scientific research. Two key concepts that lie that lie at the core of this issue comprise The Drake Equation and the Fermi Paradox.

The chapter below will provide a brief overview of these theories, while evaluating the possibility of locating alien life.

The Drake Equation: A Numerical Method to Estimating Alien Life

It is the probabilistic Drake Equation, developed by Dr. Frank Drake in 1961 determines the total number of communicative, active alien civilizations in the Milky Way galaxy. The equation reads:

N = R* x fp x ne x fl x fi x fc x L

Where:

N is the number of civilisations within our galaxy that communicate with each other. be possible

R* = the mean speed at which star formation occurs each year in our galaxy.

fp = The percentage of the stars with the planetary system

NEE = The mean amount of celestial bodies which could sustain life star with planets

Fl is the percentage of planets with the capacity to support the development of life. develop life

fi is the fraction of the planets that have life. develop to be intelligent (civilizations)

Fc is the fraction of civilisations who develop technology capable of emitting visible indicators of their presence space

L = The length of time during which civilizations send detectable signals out into space

The Drake Equation provides an equation for estimating the potential number of communicating extraterrestrial civilisations. However, it's important to realize that the equation is based on a variety of uncertain factors. Thus, the equation serves as an ideal starting point for discussions and discussions about the possibility of alien life, but not the definitive answer.

The Fermi Paradox: Where Is Everybody?

Drake Equation is a contradiction. Drake Equation contradicts the Fermi Paradox that was named in honor of the scientist Enrico Fermi. What is the reason why hasn't the Drake Equation's predictions of numerous other alien civilizations actually been proved?

A number of fundamentals support several fundamentals that underpin Fermi Paradox:

Numerous stars in the galaxy are millions of years older than our solar system.

There are stars with Earth-like planets as well as some that may be able to cultivate intelligent life.

In spite of their slow speeds they should have had plenty of time to discover and explore the universe, considering how old the galaxy is.

So far, we do not find evidence of extraterrestrial existence.

Possible Solutions to the Fermi Paradox

Each explanation for the paradox is based on assumptions and their implications. Some common explanations include:

1. The rare Earth Hypothesis The theory asserts that the conditions of intelligent life are unique and could be exclusive to Earth. The distance from the Sun and the existence of a huge moon as well as the presence of

plate tectonics could be a factor in Earth's ability to sustain life in conscious form and be unique throughout the universe.

2. The Great Filter could be a key barrier, or set of hurdles which prevents civilizations from reaching an advanced level in technology required for interstellar travel and communications. It is possible that the Great Filter could be something from the past, suggesting that we've already overcome an uncommon and difficult obstacle but it may also refer to the future of our species which suggests that the survival of humanity is at risk.

3. The Zoo Hypothesis The Zoo Hypothesis: This theory is that aliens have a sense of humanity, but are deciding not to communicate with us. It is possible that they are viewing us in the same way as zoo animal and they might not interfere with lesser-developed civilizations.

4. The Transcension Hypothesis The Transcension Hypothesis: It argues that

advanced civilizations could "transcend" the realm of physical reality into a different dimension. The technology we have today would be unable to be able to detect these entities.

Assessing the Probability of Discovering Extraterrestrial Life

The probability of locating life from space is difficult because of the size of the universe as well as the unknown components.

Recent advances in astronomy and the identification of a large number of exoplanets have increased excitement in searching for life in the universe beyond Earth.

Scientists are constantly improving their knowledge of the various variables that make up the Drake Equation.

Exoplanets have helped improve estimates of the habitable planets in our galaxy. Astrobiology has enriched our understanding of the world's conditions, which allows us to imagine the life of distant planets.

Despite all these advances, many issues remain unanswered. It is still a bit of a mystery knowledge of the process by which life first began to develop on Earth and if similar events may take place in other planets. It is also unclear if the development of life that is intelligent, and the capacity to communicate or move through space is unanswered.

The distance between the stars as well as technological constraints hinder searching for life beyond our planet. Finding signs of life on planets far away is not an easy task. If life is present somewhere else, we don't possess the tools to be able to see the existence of life. Science and technology have made it easier to search for other life.

Space missions like NASA's James Webb Space Telescope and European Space Agency's PLATO (PLAnetary Oscillations and Transits of Stars) mission. Oscillations of Stars) mission seek to improve our understanding of exoplanets' properties and ability to provide life support in all way.

Because of the numerous undiscovered situations and vastness of space and the universe and the vastness of space, making an accurate prediction about the likelihood of finding life from space is extremely difficult. It is difficult to determine the likelihood of finding alien life. Drake Equation and the Fermi Paradox give two distinct views on the probability of discovering intelligent life that is beyond Earth.

The Fermi Paradox asks why we aren't finding any alien civilisations despite Drake Equation's predictions of a variety. There are several theories to consider. Rare Earth Hypothesis, Great Filter, Zoo Hypothesis, and Transcension Hypothesis are fascinating Fermi Paradox solutions.

The current knowledge and technologies can't confirm or debunk these assertions.

While we travel through the universe and discover more about our own environment, we could discover other life forms. Searching for life beyond Earth is among the sciences' most exciting and difficult research areas.

Sodom and Gomorrah: A Timeless Account of Extraterrestrial Involvement?

The Old Testament story of Sodom and Gomorrah is an awe-inspiring story. They were likely found within Jordan's Ghor or valley in Jordan.

God's fury destroyed these cities the tale has been read various ways.

A fascinating theory suggests angels who came to these cities could have been aliens. The theory also suggests that nuclear blasts could destroy Sodom as well as Gomorrah.

I'll briefly look at the Biblical account, and then consider the possibility that modern technologies from the distant past played an important role in the events depicted.

The Book of Genesis tells how two angels visited Sodom. Sodom. They told Lot an honest person who helped these "angels" (or"agents" from another dimension) "agents") in the past warning that the evil cities in Sodom and Gomorrah would soon be demolished. Angels suggested Lot as well as his entire family members to get out of the city and to not return because God was planning to burn them down to dust. When the family fled and fled, a blaze of smoke and fire came down upon Sodom and Gomorrah which killed all that lived in the area.

The belief that angels of the tale are extraterrestrial beings stems from the belief. The evidence for this belief is being seen everywhere, this theory is that advanced civilizations might be visiting Earth in the past, and influenced the history of humanity and its culture.

The visitors, who were armed with a wealth of knowledge and technological expertise they could have been misinterpreted. The people of the time could have viewed the visitors as divine messengers, or angels.

In relation to Sodom and Gomorrah the angels' task to warn Lot may suggest an intervention from the outside. The supernatural power of their angels and the foresight of a looming catastrophe could suggest that they weren't just supernatural agents. In fact, they may be intelligent beings who had profound knowledge of earth's natural processes.

The devastating fall from Sodom and Gomorrah depicted as a flood of fire and sulfur. The account of the consequences of the towns is strikingly similar to the effects of a nuclear bomb. Extreme heat, burning infernos and the widespread destruction that resulted from such an incident are in line with the Biblical depiction of destruction to cities.

The close resemblance between the story of the destruction of Sodom and Gomorrah to a contemporary nuclear blast makes us believe that the explosive explosion of two nuclear artifacts actually occurred at the time.

"Angels," or "angels" (or "secret aliens" placed these nuclear objects into the city to explode in the future. Thus, theorists (I myself included) think that the event was orchestrated by aliens because no other human being at the time could have this type of technology.

The long-lasting effects of radiation that is present in the area including the high sulfur and salt concentrations may support this hypothesis. They have been observed within regions like the Dead Sea region. The instructions the angels sent the angels to Lot as well as his loved ones members not to turn back can be interpreted as a message of warning. It could also be a reference to the blinding light or the harmful radiation that nuclear blasts releases.

The idea that aliens have visited Earth during the past is not a new idea. This suggests that they exchanged their knowledge and advanced technology with the earliest civilisations. People who support this theory argue that evidence for advanced technology can be found in old writing.

The theory of the Ancient Alien includes the mention of flying machines and powerful weapons. This is even mentioned found in the Bible.

The devastation of Sodom and Gomorrah as well as the possible distant origins of angels could be another illustration. The destruction of Gomorrah could be evidence of the wisdom of old, which is reflected into a Biblical account.

If viewed from the perspective of extraterrestrial interaction and the latest technology, the narrative that tells the story of Sodom and Gomorrah is a compelling new perception. While we keep examining the ancient writings and seeking answers to our deepest inquiries, we must remain open to different theories and possible interpretations. At the end of the day, the story that tells the story of Sodom and Gomorrah is when viewed through the lens of influences from outside will encourage us to dig deeper into the past's mystery and to consider the part of otherworldly creatures that they could be playing in shaping the course of our civilization.

Chapter 20: The Apocryphal Book Of Enoch

The Book of Enoch is an antiquated Jewish sacred text. It was written in around the 2nd century BCE.

It provides detailed information about the apocalyptic visions that were seen by the figure of Enoch and was elevated to heaven, where he was shown the divine information regarding angels, demons and the beginnings of humankind. The text was written in Aramaic however, it is now available with a few fragmentary versions that have been translated into various languages. While it's not included in the canon of biblical scriptures that is accepted by the majority of Judaism or Christianity Some earlier Christian religious sects as well as modern scholars remain awestruck by the book because of its special insight into pre-flood times and the angelic mythology.

Its vivid depictions of heaven's kingdoms and mysterious creatures have long attracted the interest of scholars and religious minded people.

In this piece we'll look into possible evidence that suggests the fallen celestial beings within the Enochian Manuscript were extraterrestrial travelers.

The story of fallen angels is one of the fascinating elements of the film.

The Enochian Manuscript depicts a gathering of celestial creatures known as the Watchers. They are opposed to the Almighty and then fall back into Earth to be with humanity (and when you say "fallen," you may recognize "landed"). The celestial beings of the night bestow a variety of capabilities, skills and es upon the world. However, they are also a source of danger. presence can increase violence, degrade and vice (which may be the flawed interpretation of the religious writer).

The Watchers have a mateship with human females and give birth to Nephilim which are hybrid offspring which causes chaos throughout Earth.

I'll refer to the Book of Enoch the 6th chapter, versicle 6 and Chapter 8:

"And they were all two hundred, and they ascended during the time of Jared at the top of Mount Hermon, and they identified it as Mount Hermon because they had swear 7 and bind them by mutual imprecations to the summit. The names of their chiefs: Samlazaz, their leader, Araklba, Rameel, Kokablel Tamlel, Ramlel, Danel, Ezeqeel, Baraqijal, 8. Asael and Armaros. Batarel, Ananel, Zaqiel Samsapeel Satarel, Turel, Jomjael, Sariel. These are their top leaders of 10s.

[Chapter 7]

1 All the other together took to themselves wives, and every picked one for themselves They began to join them, and to smear their bodies with them. And they taught them charms and enchantments, as well as the cutting of the roots. They also they

introduced them to the vegetation. Then they were pregnant and bear giants of great size, which were 3000 ells. They devoured all the possessions of humankind. When men were unable to be able to sustain them any longer and the giants became angry, they resisted five of them and devoured humanity. Then they started to commit sins against animals, birds reptiles, birds, and six fish. They ate each other's flesh and drink their blood. The earth then laid a charge against the unruly ones.

[Chapter 8]

1 Then Azazel taught men how to make knives and swords as well as shields and breastplates, and taught them the various metals found in the earth as well as how to work on them. They also made bracelets as well as ornaments, the application of antimony as well as the beautification of the eyeslids and other types of expensive stones as well as all two coloring tinctures. Then there was much wickedness as well as

fornication as well as being misled and turned unclean in all ways. Semjaza was a teacher of enchantments and root-cuttings. 'Armaros was the resolution of magical enchantments. Baraqijal (taught) the astrology system as well as Kokabel's constellations. Ezeqeel the wisdom of the clouds, the Earth's signs, Shamsiel the signs of the sun and Sariel the direction of the moon's course."

What do you think it is like to you? Does it seem like spiritual Angels have to "fornicate" to women? IMHO they were aliens who were no as different as us, because they gathered the gorgeous women from the earthlings and then married their beautiful wives. These "giants," who were their sons, might be figuratively speaking in that they could be blessed with more power thanks to their more advanced genetics.

Returning to the conservative view, Examining the parallels with the ancient writings and contemporary UFO sightings.

The notion that the lost heaven-bound creatures might have been aliens who explorers originates from similarities in its illustrations and the reports of contemporary UFO encounters. The Watchers possess advanced knowledge and technologies, educating humanity about abilities previously unimaginable. The idea has a lot in common with the idea that extraterrestrials could have been on Earth early in time and passed on their wisdom to the ancient civilizations.

Additionally there is there is the Nephilim idea, which was created by the Watchers as well as the mating of females by humans, is a reference to tales of human-alien fusion and genetic mutations. The connections are causing many to suggest about the possibility that Enochian Manuscript may be documenting contact with other life forms from the universe.

The cosmonaut theory of the past states that alien species visited Earth in the past. They have influenced many aspects of our society.

The theory has been linked to The Enochian Manuscript. According to those who support this idea, the ancient cultures usually depicted gods as well as otherworldly entities as celestial travelers, maybe reflecting real contact with other species.

The impact of the Enochian Manuscript's story on popular culture as well as UFOlogy can be seen for certain. The narrative of the Watchers as well as the Nephilim is the basis for a number of films, literature as well as television. The Watchers are constantly investigating the notion that the ancient texts could be a clue to the existence of aliens.

It is crucial to look at different interpretations of this Enochian Manuscript and its depictions of fallen angels. There are those who claim that the text can be described more as a work of symbolism and mythology instead of a true account of events in the past.

Some critics of the extraterrestrial theory argue that there is no any evidence that proves the fall of divine beings of the night were not aliens.

In spite of the differing opinion, it's important to be open towards the subject.

The Enochian Manuscript provides an enthralling insight into old beliefs and concepts. Looking into the possibility of contact with aliens increases our understanding of the texts.

The Enochian Manuscript and its description of fallen gods provide the opportunity to explore the possible connections between old literature as well as alien realities. It is important to conduct the investigation with a sense of prudence and skepticism The parallels that exist between the Watchers and the Nephilim and the more recent UFO encounters provide a fascinating base for further research and discussion. In the end, the Enochian Manuscript captivates our imaginations by beckoning us to delve deeper into the mysteries of our past as well as the possibilities of UFO visits.

UFO sightings that could be possible from ancient times, prior to the advent of planes

From historical sources as well as religious texts and mythology, I'll provide UFO sightings that could have occurred since the beginning of times. These were prior to the time that planes flew in the skies were a common event (except for the very last):

1. Nuremberg celestial phenomenon (1561) The inhabitants from Nuremberg, Germany, reported having seen various objects appear within the sky, which included globes, cylinders and crosses. The incident was reported in the local paper, including a woodcut depicting the mysterious phenomena.

2. Alexander The Great's "Flying Shields" (329 BC): The legend goes that at the time of Alexander the Great's battles his troops witnessed "flying shields" which emitted flash of light that caused anxiety among troops.

3. The vision of Ezekiel's "Wheel within the wheel" (593 BC): The Bible book of Ezekiel provides a description of the concept of a "wheel inside an wheel" with four living things, which is believed to be an indication of a UFO sighting.

4. Old Cave Paintings (prehistoric time) Many cave paintings from all over the world depict characters as well as objects which resemble contemporary descriptions of UFOs and extraterrestrials. Examples are the Tassili n'Ajjer National Park in Algeria and the Sego Canyon in Utah, USA.

5. It is the Vimanas (ancient India): Ancient Indian texts including the Mahabharata as well as the Ramayana are about flying machines, also known as "vimanas" which can travel across the sky and in space. Many believe that these could be UFOs or other technology from the universe.

6. Roman "Phantom ship" (218 BC): Livy the Roman historian, was a witness and wrote about the "Phantom ship" which was

observed through the air at the time by an impressive amount of people.

7. The phenomenon of the celestial in Japan (1235) The story goes like this: A mysterious light appeared across the sky of Japan and was accompanied by strange objects that resembled "ears from rice." The phenomenon was scrutinized by the General Yoritsume and concluded that it was caused by winds.

8. The Flaming Shields of Miletus (214 BC) A. Greek historian Phlegon of Tralles reported an incident in which "flaming shields" could be seen in skies over the city of Miletus which is now Turkey.

9. "UFO Battle," or the "UFO Battle" in Nuremberg (1566) Akin to 1561's event A second sighting took place within Nuremberg in 1566. In Nuremberg, witnesses reported seeing a variety of UFOs in the sky that appeared to fight.

10. The Miracle of the Sun (1917) Though necessarily "ancient," this event was recorded

before the advent of airplanes. It was in Fatima, Portugal, thousands of people were able to witness that the sun "dance" across the sky before changing color which was later declared an act of God in authorities of the Catholic Church. Many believe that this could be an UFO sighting.

We'll go deeper into each of them individually in the sections in this chapter.

You are free to skip the next chapter if they do not appeal to you.

Nuremberg Celestial Phenomenon (1561)

The Nuremberg Celestial Phenomenon in 1561 saw a large number of celestial phenomenon or unknown floating objects (UFOs) in the skies above Nuremberg which was one of the Free Imperial City of the Holy Roman Empire at the time. In the early morning of April 14th 1561, several males and females in Nuremberg reported seeing an aerial combat "out of the sunlight." This event was reported in a broadsheet newspaper story published in the month of the month of April 1561. The article included woodcut illustrations as well as a text written from Hans Glaser.

The paper, which measures 26.2 centimeters (10.3 inches) by 38.0 centimeters (15.0 inches) It is stored in the collections at the Library of Zurich in Zurich, Switzerland.

Based on the broadsheet, the large black object was seen after the aerial fight. The exhausted spheres of combatants were tossed down to earth amid clouds of smoke. People who witnessed the incident reported seeing hundreds of cylinders, spheres, and various other strangely-shaped objects soaring around over the air. The illustration of woodcuts shows a variety of forms, such as crosses (with or without spheres on their arms) smaller spheres, two huge crescents, a spear of black, as well as circular objects. Then, a few small spheres emerged, and then dipped across the sky in the early morning light.

Writer Jason Colavito notes that the broadsheet of wood became well-known within the modern world after it was released in Carl Jung's 1958 publication, Flying Saucers: A Modern Myth of Things Seen in the Skies. Jung believed the event could be to be a natural phenomenon that had theological and military implications encircling the phenomenon. He believed that the spectacle could be like the swarm of insects that rise in the sun, if UFOs were living creatures. They'd mate, and they'd rejoice at the wedding flight.

The engraving made of wood.

The people who lived in those days didn't have any idea of aircrafts, starships, or missiles, the only option they'd think of was exactly what they saw in the movie in the movie, even though they might observe a contemporary dogfight among fighter aircraft. IMHO could be evidence of the war between two powers from space on the earth.

Think about it: an extended period of time between this "battle" as well as the second battle, also in Nurenberg In 1566, the world was beginning to move past the darkness and into Renaissance. It seems that our planet is now owned by different people. That's how I'm able to think of to convey this. The previous owner was discovered in the dark ages as well as Inquisition and the power of the church in manipulating individuals. These newer owners are more accommodating to our development which allows us to develop and rise to the top of the mountain. For them, I send my "Thank for your time' to the people who won the battles.

Many believe that some consider the Nuremberg Celestial Phenomenon of 1561 as a possible sun dog sighting, an occurrence that is natural. There is also speculation that it could be UFO-related. It is undetermined and speculation.

Alexander the Great's "Flying Shields"Alexander the Great is frequently considered to be a symbol of power, grandeur, expertise, and victory. But, he was also among the greatest conquerors throughout the world of antiquity. His troops fought several battles and was consistently able to win victories. But, one particular incident that occurred during his conquest of modern Uzbekistan during 329 BC stand out. The event included "flying shields."

In the work of historian Arrian, Anabasis Alexandri. Alexander encountered a series of airborne objects as he traveled along the Jaxartes River (also known as the Syr Darya). The objects, which resembled shields, appeared from the air in a thin layer. They were said to have surrounded Alexander and his army for some time before disappearing out into the night.

As it was written nearly two centuries following the event it is doubtful as to its authenticity. But, a variety of theories are being offered to explain the bizarre event.

Many speculated that it might be an astronomical phenomenon such as the meteor shower. Other researchers consider the possibility of unusual atmospheric phenomena that causes the light to reflect in unique patterns.

A different theory points to earlier experiments using hot air balloons conducted by Persian priests as the reason for"flying shields" sightings "flying shields" sightings. If this is the case, the primitive balloons could have been made out of fabric, then filled using hydrogen. They could be tied together in a remote location to create the appearance of a hovering or flying construction.

In contrast certain ufologists believe that the event was the result of the encounter of extraterrestrial types. They believe that the shields that flew around were in reality, UFOs which were that were visiting the planet.

They remain mysterious and keep us thinking about them regardless of the interpretation. The Alexander mystery is a hot topic of debate experiences over 2500 years later.

It's fascinating to consider that stories of UFO sightings have been reported in many other civilizations throughout the course of human history.

From the earliest Egyptian hieroglyphs, to Renaissance art to the current rumours of encounters with aliens, the idea of aliens coming to Earth has always intrigued people.

There is no clear answer is available to explain the events Alexander discovered in Uzbekistan in the year 329 BC. There is no evidence to support the existence of extraterrestrials, however this fascinating story has stood the examination of time.

Ezekiel's "Wheel inside wheel" (593 BC)

One of the most intriguing stories from ancient texts is one from the Book of Ezekiel. The prophet reveals a complex creature known as the "Wheel inside a Wheel." In Ezekiel's story dating to the year 593 BC, the prophet experienced visions. A strange and unnatural vessel fell from the sky during the vision.

The account in question is one of numerous historical sources that hint at encounters with technology that is advanced or other life forms. The account given by Ezekiel is similar to modern reports on UFO sightings.

The wheels are described as composed of multiple components and spinning at a rapid rate. They're adorned with eye-shaped rims that are that have been used for millennia to represent cameras or windows.

In addition, there was mention of objects made of metal hanging over the wheels.

There are many interpretations of the exact events that were seen by Ezekiel

There are theories that suggest the existence of the presence of ancient astronauts on Earth and others argue that the vision could be symbolic and didn't have any relation to the real world.

As an ufologist who carefully studied the history of records that have mysterious phenomenon, I am curious about how well-versed some are to the description of crafts. There are reports of rotating disks, surrounded by lights that span our skies in the present.

There are ongoing debates over whether the sighting is actually depicting alien technology or whether the sighting had a spiritual significance the only thing that cannot be debated is the significance of historic events. The story of Ezekiel's "Wheel inside the Wheel" is undeniably influential on many religions and cultures across the ages.

A lot of ufologists believe that the explanations that are provided by Ezekiel give a clear image of aliens from another planet that utilize modern technology. If you believe in this idea the account of Ezekiel certainly encourages people to think differently regarding the interpretation of historical events, and examining alternatives to conventional explanations of mysterious phenomena.

To conclude, although there isn't a definitive evidence or a consensus on the visions that prophet Ezekiel observed, it's undisputed that it was a powerful event. The imagery of the prophet fascinates us nowadays and prompts questions regarding how humans have confronted ideas which aren't part of the realm of our understanding. It's also essential for connecting communities with identical stories over time, crucial for the social task at hand.

Antiquated Cave Drawings (prehistoric time):

Through time, humankind has always been intrigued by the idea of the existence of aliens and their potential visits to Earth.

Although modern science is yet confirmed that intelligent life exists in the universe, a number of old cave paintings from all over the world depict images and objects which resemble modern descriptions of aliens as well as UFOs.

An example is located within Tassili n'Ajjer National Park in Algeria. These cave paintings depict creatures with long heads big eyes and slim bodies, these are all traits commonly associated with extraterrestrials. The paintings could have been created as early as 6000 BCE far before any contact was made with any other civilization.

Similar to that, Sego Canyon in Utah has petroglyphs that depict bizarre humanoid characters with large heads and huge eyes. Barrier Canyon in Utah features similar depictions.

In addition, what appears as flying saucers, or some other unknown objects hovering above the figures.

The cave paintings from the past were discovered at Chhattisgarh, India, stretching to more than 10,000 years.

They are believed as being among the oldest. The drawings show humanoids sporting suits and helmets while performing various tasks including hunting, farming, or agriculture. Researchers think that they could be astronauts from another planet who came to our planet from prehistoric times.

Although these are only one of many that have been discovered across the globe, suggesting encounters with aliens These have sparked discussions. Both researchers and UFO aficionados discuss these occurrences. There are those who believe that the representations are simply symbolic or depict figures of religion. But some believe they are unmistakable evidence of the ancient interaction with creatures from various worlds.

The primary reason behind similarities between cave paintings from different regions of the world may be the result of cultural exchanges or migration routes. When viewed separately it is difficult to figure out how early people were able to create similar images. Although they were separated geographically by vast distances, these illustrations were a representation of mysterious animals and other creatures similar to modern UFOs. It's the reason a lot of scientists find it fascinating and intriguing.

In addition, there's a substantial archaeological evidence to support these reports of sightings. It ranges from stone age metallic sculptures that were discovered in the central plain of Colombia, similar to what we consider spaceships today, to the incredibly deep tunnels that were discovered beneath the Peru's Sacsayhuaman Temple complex. They are like nothing you've ever previously seen on Earth.

It is a matter of opinion, regardless of whether you believe that aliens from the past walked our planet before the time of prehistoric civilization or whether the depictions are a reflection of our imaginations at play, these works can be said to stimulate an introspective thought. They prompt us to rethink the accepted mythologies and encourage the acceptance of diverse views about our history.

Chapter 21: The Vimanas Were Ancient Flying Machines From The Past Of India

The enigmatic Vimanas is a subject of fascination for old astronauts as well as UFO fans for a long time. The Vimanas could provide proof of alien visits to Earth.

The flying vehicle was featured in Indian epics such as the Ramayana as well as the Mahabharata. The text described how they could fly through the air using the power of propulsion.

According to mythology that the Vimanas were not just devices but were advanced technology developed by gods, or even extraterrestrial beings. In the end, they were able to move at incredible speed and make maneuvers unimaginable for human-made machines at the time.

Some ufologists believe that the description about Vimanas within these stories might represent evidence of aliens from the past traveling through our planet. Indeed, some scientists consider that Vimanas may have been ancient planes piloted by alien creatures. They may have were on Earth to impart knowledge to the humans.

The most intriguing aspect that is fascinating about this Vimana legend is its resemblance with UFO sightings of the present day similar to stories of flying objects that are not identified and accounts of Vimanas frequently include mentions of a sky filled with lights. Also, they mention bizarre flying maneuvers which defy conventional knowledge of aerodynamics. Additionally, a lot of Vimana stories involve encounters with powerful entities equipped with the latest technology. They can perform amazing feats that seem to be impossible, much similar to modern stories of abductions from aliens.

Some skeptical people could dismiss Vimana tales as just stories or myths, the ancient space theorists have numerous evidences to support this. In particular, the details of Vimanas in texts from the past often contain information that could be considered to represent technological advancements or spacecraft from the stars. Furthermore, numerous instances of the ancient world talk about strange flying objects, or entities. This has been associated with encounters with extraterrestrial beings.

There is no definitive support for the notion that Vimanas are evidence of earlier extraterrestrial visits. Yet, similar descriptions of advanced aircrafts and alien-like beings in legends and myths all over the world suggest that the stories could be true. To conclude, the Vimana myths remain fascinating topics for discussion with ancient astronaut theorists and UFO enthusiasts alike.

Although it's difficult to know the truth of whether these aircrafts were really evidence of beings from another world visiting the planet, it is clear that the concept of advanced technology and extinct creatures have been a part of our culture since the beginning of time. Be it fact or myth stories of Vimanas provide interesting insights into the history of our world. Unsolved mysteries that remain to be the public are truly fascinating.

The Roman "Phantom Ship"

The events of the year 218 BC just off of Sicily is commonly referred to as "The Roman Phantom Ship."

According to Roman historian Titus Livius (Livy), in his work "Ab Urbe Condita" (i.e., "The Roman History,"" Chapter 21 Chapter 62) A mysterious vessel was suddenly visible at the top of the sky. Literally speaking, in Latin it read: "vanadium speciem de caelo adfulsisse" that in English signifies "Phantom ships were observed glinting through the night skies."

It was heading toward Rome's naval fleet in the Second Punic War. Despite efforts to stop the ship, and even firing flaming bows into its sails the ghost ship continued to sail in its course without damaging anything and slowed down.

Although some think this incident is a legend or myth Some speculate it may indicate that extraterrestrials have a hand into human affairs. Ufologists believe that aliens been on Earth at times in the past and have influenced the human civilization. They did this via creating myths and stories like the one of ghost ships, or perhaps direct involvement in conflicts among nations.

Though there isn't any evidence that supports the theories, a lot of people enjoy these stories. It is due to the fact that stories of similar events have been found in various cultures across the world. Examples include similar legends of ghost ship apparitions across Norse mythology, and Caribbean ghost tales exist.

Additionally, some texts portray the existence of beings that have advanced technology which are beyond the capabilities of human beings. For instance, the Indian epic poem "Ramayana" is a description of flying machines known as Vimanas. These were utilized by gods as well as other gods and beings of power for sky transportation to fulfill their purposes.

In spite of debates over whether aliens been to Earth and other unanswered mysteries of the past still enthral people throughout time. It doesn't matter if these are true or historical events like the Roman Empire's Phantom Ship, humanity still is fascinated by mysterious events from the past.

The bottom line is that what occurred off the coast of Sicily in the past centuries is not yet known. However, what is certain is that curiosity about unresolved events has influenced generations.

The Celestial Phenomenon over Japan

In 1235, a bizarre celestial phenomenon took place at Nishinomiya, Japan. Based on historical accounts witnesses claimed to have seen the flaming object flying through the skies. The object then split into many pieces before disappearing into the nearby mountains.

Some historians attribute the event due to a meteor or comet sighting, other researchers speculate in a different way. Some think there might exist more to this tale than a natural phenomenon.

One possibility for explaining one possible explanation for Celestial Phenomenon over Japan is that it is actually the first UFO sighting. Theorists of the past suggest that extraterrestrials could have been on Earth in various times throughout the course of history. They suggest that they had an impact on human civilization and culture in ways that are still evident today.

The people who support this theory believe that various cultures of the past have left stories and myths. They tell stories of encounters with supernatural beings, or technological advancements such as flying saucers, or Vimanas. Vimanas are old Indian flying machines mentioned in Hindu texts written thousands of years ago.

Additionally, artifacts from the ago often portray what seem as modern-day airplanes. Of course the fact is that this was happening before humans have discovered these aircrafts, and some skeptics also believe in that it's just a coincidence.

There is no way to pinpoint exactly what caused this Celestial Phenomenon over Japan in 1235. The possibility of an alien influence is an explanation that could be a part of the various scientific theories including meteorites and comets. Humanity is always fascinated by mysterious mysteries that are not explained. This includes sightings of undetected floating objects (UFOs) and crops that have circles in them as well as deep underground phenomena that are beyond logic. Because our understanding is limited, this leads to discussions about theories linking them to aliens that have entered Earth in space.

The need to be open-minded is paramount when research continues to investigate the mysterious phenomena and researchers are still searching for the answers. It is important to recognize that there exist physical manifestations that are out of our reach, waiting to be unraveled by scientists.

The Flaming Shields of Miletus

The Flaming Shields of Miletus is an old incident that has baffled scientists, experts, and historians for a long time. As part of a battle in two empires, the Seleucid Empire as well as the Ptolemaic Kingdom, in the year the year 214 BC The troops of Miletus, the capital city Miletus were able to report a stunning incident. They saw shields rising towards the sky, with flames radiating out of their tops. They then dived down to the opposite groups.

Although some people dismiss it as folklore or mythology numerous experts argue that the sighting is akin to reports of mysterious flying objects (UFOs) across the ages. Additionally, these sightings are documented in records from the past of numerous civilizations around the globe.

The phenomenon is generating renewed interest for those who believe the existence of extraterrestrials is possible. This curiosity extends beyond up to today, but into the past. The evidence suggests that inhabitants of other worlds or civilizations may have traveled out of the solar system. But, the theories remain unproven without any evidence.

Similar accounts to the shields that exploded have been recorded in other times of the past. Lights could be seen flying around or dropping down at staggering speeds with bizarre patterns, often not in accordance with the natural movements. For instance, examples of hovering, zigzagging and flying with no apparent mechanism or propeller system. Also, descriptions like "navigating with no using oars" have been reported to be appearing several times in different old records.

This evidence strongly suggests that the existence of something that is beyond human understanding occurred during that time. It could be hard to grasp today given the absence of technology in the past.

The interpretations of each person are different and some believe that coincidences are the norm, and others rely on the evidence of circumstantial sources. The resemblance between diverse cultures' accounts of extraordinary aerial sights could suggest that it's other than imagination is that is at work. In all the time this story suggests an even deeper reality that which we aren't able to fully grasp.

While we aren't certain about its precise kind of nature but the Flaming Shields sighting in Miletus remains fascinating. It has captured the imagination of people over the past millennia, and offers a an intriguing glimpse of our time. It reveals the possibility of UFO reports dating to the beginning of time.

The notion of the influence of aliens on the human story is one of the most fascinating ideas for the human race. Is it the case that aliens have was on Earth during antiquity, had an impact on the early human civilizations or even played an influence on some crucial historic instances? These theories have drawn interest from both academics and fans alike, who are enthralled by the possibilities that might be more to it than meets the eye of an individual.

There are many who remain skeptical despite a variety of theories that have been proposed through many years for explaining such events as natural phenomenon or the phenomenon of mass hyperbole. There is no evidence to prove either theory.

The "UFO Battle" in 1566 Nuremberg 1566.

Early in the morning on 14 April 1566, people living in Nuremberg, Germany, witnessed the event that is now referred to by the name of "UFO Battle." Based on eyewitness reports, numerous unidentified flying objects were seen over the city. They then began an intense fight.

In this eerie incident, witnesses reported seeing objects like orbs as well as disc-like shapes. The two parties engaged in an intense aerial battle that lasted for several minutes until they vanished completely. The skies erupted with unimaginable strength, frightening people in their houses. Then they realized that they'd witnessed something far greater than just an normal day-to-day incident.

In spite of little or no news coverage at the time with limited communication, there were soon rumors were circulated of strange reports of sightings. The sightings were reported across nearby countries, and even frightened high-end army units with no reason or direction. Modern historians believe that those sighting reports may be a factor in battle plans for the coming century's war scenarios. This demonstrates the significance and significance of events at the time.

As written records were not common at the time, it's challenging for many researchers today to study the past's existence. The absence of evidence suggests some theories that are based on long-standing myths of different culture. There are theories that suggest possible scientific explanations that fit into a pre-existing structure, that is in contradiction to modern conventional practices.

The evidence supports similar brainwashed conditions prevalent during times when the orthodox religion beliefs often blocked similar studies by claiming they were directly in opposition to God.

But, those who support it claim that the medieval events could have been evidence of technological advancements in extraterrestrial conflicts. This idea is especially plausible when you consider other historical proof that dates back to the past centuries, indicating the regular interaction between humanity as well as beings from other planets.

A lot of ufologists believe that extraterrestrials who had superior intelligence could have been on Earth during the past. They could have passed on their wisdom to humanity and helped us advance our technology. It is believed that the UFO Battle of Nuremberg could provide another instance of interaction between human beings and alien civilisations.

It's also fascinating to examine the UFO combat with similar incidents in the past, since it is fun. As an example, UFO sightings were observed near large lakes, lakes and oceans. These are which are known to store the most energy in Earth. There is speculation that this could be a crucial requirement for the advanced aliens that allows simple landings and elevated levels off of planets for an easy replenishment of supplies that are not accessible in other places.

It cannot be determined with certainty what transpired at the time of the "UFO Battle" in Nuremberg in 1566. However, many experts are of the opinion that this historical incident remains unsolved. Many skeptical scientists dismiss UFO sightings as merely meteorological phenomenon or pranks perpetrated by local pranksters theories that allow for a critical analysis of evidence that points to extraterrestrial activity can't completely exclude the possibility of paranormal phenomena. This is due to the necessity of more definitive proof that is negative and challenges rational explanations that are unable to comprehend all of the elements that are associated with the sightings, or even in the various cultures of all time.

Whatever one's opinions are about theories of astronauts or life that extends beyond the boundaries of our planet there is no way to avoid the fact that stories such as "The UFO Battle" concerning Nuremberg remain a major draw for people around the world. Believers as well as skeptics get involved in new debates and pursuit of a greater knowledge of the possible participation they've previously been pursuing for centuries not being recognized.

The "Miracle of the Sun" in Fatima, Portugal

On the 13th October 1917, hundreds of people gathered at Fatima, Portugal, to watch what's known as"The Miracle of the Sun. According to the testimony of those present at the celebration The sun was seen to appear within the sky. After that, it sank rapidly to Earth prior to returning to its original location.

Although many believe this is due to divine intervention or extraordinary event linked to religion Some experts offer a different theory. The evidence could point to alien activity that closely matches the popular phenomenon known as unidentified flying objects, or UFOs.

The paranormality of these reports has led to speculation and debates for a long time. In all likelihood, there are a lot of accounts from different eras that have similar phenomena to the "dancing sun" that last over long periods of time appear. One can only wonder if the possibility of something beyond an imagination. It's interesting enough!

There are some researchers who believe that because the latest technology was either difficult to access for the majority of people in the past the aliens' presence could be hidden behind religions. These supernatural phenomena were directly attributed to gods.

Could it be that the those who claim to have witnessed miracles may actually be the sightings of spacecrafts from other planets? With our current knowledge of planets that sustainably live living spaces that are habitable inside as well as outside of the solar system this possibility isn't entirely unthinkable.

While many are still unsure whether aliens have visited Earth in the past, due to the absence of any direct evidence evidence, those who support the theory argue for the existence of evidence from circumstantial sources. Additionally, the resemblance between historical evidence from various cultures suggesting the possibility of a natural, non-human movement technology suggests the possibility of earlier contacts with aliens regarded as intelligent beyond the normal limitations of human senses over previous encounters.

In this context this, the phenomenon of the sun appears to be a mystery which can't be determined conclusively. Some speculate that extraterrestrial entities being behind the blame the paranormal events while others believe they are mysterious natural phenomena or the manifestations that are related to God or divine involvement.

Whatever one's opinion in this debate It is difficult to avoid the power and fascination that mysterious occasions such as that of the Miracle of the Sun hold over the people. It is a fascination that extends to all who live in Portugal in the time and also across the generations, creating curiosity and debate that fuels an idea that there could exist more to it than what is apparent from one's eyes alone.

It is a matter of opinion whether extraterrestrials visited Fatima, Portugal, on the 13th of October 1917 the fact remains that the fact that its mystery and related phenomenon inspire people's imagination, and intrigue people, even if they lose their impact in time.

It was the Golden Age of Science Fiction and its impact in American Society and Pop CultureWithin the American cultural landscape (with the influence of the world) it is possible to be able to call"the Golden Age of Science Fiction (1934-1963) expanded its thrilling spread of tentacles. The period changed not only the realm of literary fiction, but the basis of American views of the celestial realm, space-based vessels, as well as their influence on popular culture. Science fiction went beyond its straightforward pulp roots in the period and grew into an energizing powerhouse. It infused the pages of magazines, books TV programs, novels, as well as films. The chapter explores the numerous methods Science Fiction affected American society's belief in aliens as well as the ripples they created in media and popular culture.

In the 1930s, young editors and writers sought an academic, more sensitive, and socially-conscious scientific fiction setting. The most notable writers contributed significantly throughout this Golden Age of Science Fiction. The birth of the Flash Gordon comic strip in 1934 as well as Hollywood's giants of sci-fi such as King Kong (1933) heralded the dawn of this captivating period. John W. Campbell's leadership for Astounding in 1937 further consolidated that Golden Age of Science Fiction. He helped to create a polished and significant socially conscious storytelling.

The era of the present authors created stories about the existence of extraterrestrials as well as spacecraft. They stimulated readers' imagination and stimulated a thirst to know more about life outside our globe. In the end, American society's belief in the existence of aliens as well as spaceships were profoundly affected through the work of these creative writers.

A number of pioneers, including Isaac Asimov, Robert A. Heinlein as well as Arthur C. Clarke shaped our perception of interstellar travel and cosmic life. Asimov's Foundation series and Heinlein's Stranger in a Strange Land as well as Clarke's Childhood's End were among the many influential works. They widened the reader's views of interstellar space and created curiosity to explore various other planets.

The rise of science-fiction periodicals and the growth of television film and television shows have also been a major factor.

The haphazard "movement" was a common theme in American popular culture and branched into multiple media types. They included magazines, novels television shows, and films. magazines like The Magazine of Fantasy and Science Fiction and World Science Fiction appeared. They gave writers to publish their original and thrilling stories with an audience that was larger.

Shows on television like Star Trek (1966-1969), directed by Gene Roddenberry, and Lost in Space (1965-1968) produced by Irwin Allen, captivated viewers. They featured cosmic adventures and encounters with alien species. The programs were entertaining and exposed audiences to the latest scientific theories as well as ideas regarding the cosmic sphere.

Films from this the time were The Day the Earth Stood Still (1951), The War of the

Worlds (1953) as well as Forbidden Planet (1956). The films showcased the ability of this genre to tell thrilling stories that integrated emotions of the human race with stunning visual effects at the time. The cinematic marvels fueled the desire for exploring space and possibility of communicating with alien beings. They fueled the fascination of people with spacecrafts and aliens.

The whole thing impacted American society's views on the existence of aliens and spaceships, and the impact they had on popular culture. The genre sparked curiosity and amazement about the universe, which is still present to this day. Science fiction has affected generations of filmmakers, writers as well as readers across North America and the world.

They expanded their worldviews and visualized the cosmos' endless possibilities, which led to the growth of space racing. The time of space exploration changed the world forever as people became enthralled with the expanding space program and the possibility of discovering alien life.

The Battle of Los Angeles (1942)

The Battle of Los Angeles, in the way it's known was fought in the evening of February 24-25, 1942. It was an important event, involving the alleged attack of an enemy at the city.

This event has become significant in the field of ufology because of the possibility of alien involvement and the context of World War II.

Background and Timeline of the Event

After the Pearl Harbor attack, tensions were at a high in all of the United States. At dawn, on the morning on February 25 Air raid sirens were heard across Los Angeles County. Antiaircraft guns shot at unknown objects found near Santa Monica until dawn.

Chapter 22: Eyewitness Accounts And Evidence

Military and civilians have were able to testify about strange sights in the course of this incident. The famous photo that was published by the LA Times also indicated unexplained flying objects.

The Army Air Force Headquarters confirmed that they had seen multiple metallic flying disc objects that had no distinct features in just a few 15 minutes.

Government and Military Response

The first claims of the night had an enemy plane attack Los Angeles rather than UFOs which was later eliminated as a false alarm. But, the extermination tanks traveled through three days and found no evidence of attacks on the side of the enemy or attacking American forces. A reckless or friendly fire using anti-aircraft weapons might have led to such a display.

It was reported that the US Government released "official" photos showing noticeable blips linked to the formation found over L.A. The examination revealed several tracks that began to rise to the skies after blasts fired from the aiming object. In the event that missiles missed completely they were seen with no time restriction on its rotation about the target, while simultaneously showing the aerodynamic stability as well as Aurae-like oxygenated lamps. These have been observed before using signals and were shown in detail through motion picture films as still images.

Ufological Theories and Alternative Explanations

The Battle has been suggested to be an UFO phenomenon, with a close similarities to the orbs observed in previous events. But, when looking at the photo various theories of analysis are being proposed about the size of the object or form, concluding that this UFO may not originate from Earth. Some other possible explanations for the sightings are weather balloons, massive hysteria or tests conducted by the military.

The Aztec UFO Crash: A Mysterious Incident in the New Mexico Desert (1948)

The year 1948 was when Aztec, New Mexico was featured in the news for being a potential UFO crash scene. According to various sources, an unknown flying object crashed onto Hart Canyon Ranch in the Aztec region.

In the context of one of the major historical events of Ufology and the most debated events in Ufology groups, it's now hard to differentiate the fact from fiction.

The event was first documented in the book of Frank Scully in his book "Behind The Flying Saucers." The author referred to his discussions with two men who were not known by the names "Newton" or "Chambers." They said they had the inside scoop on debris from an alien craft discovered in Hart Canyon Ranch that measured about 100 feet in size.

It appeared to be an unexploded spacecraft that was partially covered in sand and covered in pieces of debris. The rancher was said to have found some of the bones of several small humanoid animals who looked dead inside the spacecraft.

An alleged photo taken by a deceased Alien of the Aztec Crash.

They were said to be around four feet tall, were said to have huge heads and slender bodies with features that were strikingly like the typical description of what is known as "grey" extraterrestrials.

Many scholars have claimed over time that there was evidence that the Aztec UFO incident was a complex fake orchestrated by greedy individuals who wanted fame and money. Others claim that the legend was concocted by a scam person known as Silas Newton, who used this story to market his bogus oil detector.

However, despite hoax accusations many ufologists and research scientists claim their belief that Aztec UFO incident is unveiled by the government in secrets.

They argue that the fact was purposely removed from the public eye to conceal the reality and preserve the government's control over the most advanced technology from space.

While there are doubts about the veracity of these claims, and allegations against Scully of releasing sensational reports concerning UFO sightings prior to the incident (which were later proved to not be as true) Certain researchers believe that there is a element of truth in them. Based on their findings, at the very least three eyewitnesses reported that they saw something unusual flying above their heads, before crashing into adjacent land during March 25th/26th about 11 pm at night.

Notably, only a handful of scientists have backed these claims throughout time against debunkings despite many decades. By mentioning Dr. Harder and Scott Ramsey, they reject the mainstream media's attempts to discredit the evidence in support of "The Aztec Incident."

A few ufologists have proposed an possible possibility that US Air Force intercepted and concealed a real extraterrestrial wreckage. People who support this hypothesis argue that following actions of government officials and law enforcement officials point to an organized effort to cover up evidence of wreckage from an alien craft.

The website for the FBI's "Vault" was the home of"Hottel memo "Hottel memo" in April of 2011.

This letter, which circulated online over a period of time without being classified, was believed to be an evidence of the existence of a US government covering-up. It contained Guy Hottel's investigation report, as well as the FBI agent responsible for the Washington field office. The letter was addressed to J. Edgar Hoover and indexed within FBI documents, however this was a standard procedure.

Two years after it was posted after its release on the FBI site, the report was viewed more than a million times.

The Guy Hottel Memo.

The reported UFO incident that occurred in Aztecs is one of the discussed events in the history of UFOlogy and there are questions about whether this was an actual UFO sighting or just a hoax.

Contrary to the false claims Many ufologists and research scientists think that they have evidence that the Aztec UFO crash was actually an real event that was hidden in the government's secret documents.

The proponents claim that the event was intentionally disregarded to deflect attention from the facts and to protect the government's exclusive rights to superior technological advancements.

The Pioneering UFO Sighting That Coined "Flying Saucers" (1947)

On the 24th of June 1947, an American aviation expert, Kenneth Arnold, inadvertently began the current UFO the era. This incident marked a turning event in the current UFO stories. This episode heightened my interest in UFOs and extraterrestrial life.

Kenneth Arnold, an entrepreneur and private aviator, stumbled upon an unusual phenomenon while flying across Mount Rainier, Washington. That day in summer when he flew towards Yakima from Chehalis at the time that an unexpected event occurred. This event would change his entire life, and alter the course of Ufology.

Arnold was a seasoned pilot and had accumulated over 9000 hours of flying in the course of his work. But what he witnessed at the time had him enthralled in seeking out answers. The reason was that he had a lot of experience in the field of aerospace technologies.

Kenneth Arnold's encounter

The year 1947 was when Kenneth Arnold, a pilot in his aircraft close to Mount Rainier in Washington state reported experiencing the most remarkable event. According to Arnold's account the witness saw nine objects speeding through the skies at incredible speeds. This incident would eventually become one of the world's most well-known UFO sightings.

Arnold depicted these objects as having the shape of a saucer. They flew much faster than the average airplane of this era. The pilot also noted that the path of flight appeared to be unorganized and unlike the previous flights he'd witnessed.

Arnold's reaction to seeing the incident was one of disbelief and shock. Arnold immediately relayed the details the incident had revealed to the local authorities and various organisations. It also was also a source of information for Air Force intelligence personnel who then questioned him on the incident.

Although Arnold's detailed description of his experiences there were many who expressed doubt and doubted his claims. But, in the days following Arnold's account becoming known numerous other sightings of UFOs were recorded throughout America. United States. This increased curiosity about UFOs and sparked widespread fear regarding the potential risks from extraterrestrial beings.

One of the major factors that contributed to people's knowledge of the incident was the media coverage. The media sparked speculation regarding the alleged activities of extraterrestrials conducted through U.S. military. U.S. military. It only attracted more attention regardless of the fact that news outlets had a difficult time finding solid proof or long-lasting testimony from witnesses regarding these claims. It was a challenge for them to remain professional in addressing the narratives that were that were associated with these incidents.

Media Response

The event impacted the public's opinions and spurred unprecedented curiosity about UFO sightings throughout America.

After the report by Kenneth Arnold of flying objects that appeared to be aliens above Mount Rainier, Washington, on the 24th of June 1947, the response from the media was massive. The newspaper's front page had banner headlines that read "Pilot Discovers

Spacecrafts at a Spectacular speed." The event was a popular subject in newsreels as well as conversations and even with those who hadn't considered the existence of alien life in the past.

The increased awareness of the nation's issues brought global attention. Some claim to have witnessed similar events abroad. These incidents, however, were not always well-reported or were kept in government classified documents, which were forever hidden within secret vaults. The evidence disappeared from view, and the evidence seized disappearing.

The origin of the phrase "flying saucer" originates from Arnold's story as well as his selection of words. Arnold compared the motions that he observed to flying saucers that skimmed across the surface of the water. Then others began to recognize the post-event descriptions that matched features and shapes including metallic sparkle, disc-shaped appendages and erratic, unstable routes. The result was that everyone jumped into the bandwagon, naming these flying saucers!

When other witnesses came forward, adding more cases, UFO sightings became commonplace. The result was a huge variety of speculations regarding the source and intent of the UFOs. Many believed that this was an answer to the question mankind had been seeking about mysterious alien beings that visited Earth. Others were convinced that a government plot was behind large-scale distractions from important questions affecting society.

The response of the public following the Kenneth Arnold incident was crucial in raising awareness of the public. It suggested that there may exist something more than our minds beyond the planet Earth. Galaxies have endless possibilities. Evidence that supports many theories were formed into communities that came together. Technology advancement and exploration into areas that were not explored yet left unanswered questions as well as unsolved questions. Astrophysics was redefined by these events by bringing constant reminders to maintain the mind free of hubris and an inclination towards discoveries that remain undiscovered.

Impact on Modern UFO Culture

One of the major consequences of Arnold's encounter was the beginning of what's now called the current UFO time period. His public response to his reports led to an explosion of reports and sightings across the globe. The public was suddenly looking at the sky more often than they had ever done before!

With the increasing number of sightings that took place, organisations dedicated investigating and comprehending UFOs that were not identified began to appear all over the world. It included groups like MUFON (Mutual UFO Network) and MUFON (Mutual UFO Network), which is still active along with smaller groups focused on particular areas of UFO investigation.

There was a lot of disagreement about who were thrilled by this latest surge of interest in extraterrestrial life. The government quickly responded by conducting military probes like Project Blue Book. They collected data on assertions, scrutinized every sighting for proof, and tried to discover the truth of the incident. The goal was to keep people's faith levels at a high level by offering rational explanations that are ordinary or scientific explanations, but while not revealing any National Security dangers.

The official statements were issued during times of events that were complex or murky to members of the Project Blue Book crew. In certain instances they had to search for an explanation that was rational, such as the hollow Earth theories supporters communicating with each other over different continents. They tried to understand the cryptic messages from alleged beings in the sky with messages that were relayed. Sometimes they tried to disprove certain reports in order to keep the hysteria levels in check. However, allegations of lying between members as well as conspiracies that lie in international networks are still surfacing.

The significance of Arnold's vision does not only apply to the realms of ufology. It's impacted popular culture too. Numerous television and film shows and even literature are greatly affected by the event. The films depict aliens landing and sightings of them, and have captured the public's interest for decades.

It's amazing that UFOs continue to capture our interest even to this day. Even though there are contradictory theories made against the UFOs, we do question and raise our eyebrows each time we watch videos pop up on platforms or social media such as YouTube. We weigh the mainstream consensus theories against the alternative theories that are presented on the internet. The alternative theories are often lacking solid evidence that support them and can blur the lines of reasoning and causes us to look at the world in an entirely different light. But, any investigation into unusual events requires a thorough study. So, in the future, we will be able to better comprehend their past as well as the possibilities that lie beyond our current understanding.

The sighting had a huge impact on our knowledge of what is beyond world Earth. In spite of all this time studies into UFO phenomenon continues to be conducted with a fervent determination.

There is a lot of interest among people who think that higher-life creatures are awaiting to come into contact with humans.

The Roswell Incident: Origin of the Extraterrestrial Belief and the Birth of UFO Conspiracy Theories

The Roswell incident is one of the most well-known and controversial UFO events. The unidentified debris of a flying object was found on a property in Roswell, New Mexico, in July 1947. The military base in Roswell initially claimed that they found the "flying disc." Then, they retract their claim and claimed that it was part of the weather balloon.

However, despite this official explanation people believe that the government was covering the events in Roswell. Some believe something more sinister took place. It is interesting that an extensive military effort could have been enacted in order to salvage a few meteorological debris has caused a snicker among those who believe.

The event at Roswell is one of the very first assertions regarding extraterrestrial contacts in American land. This helped bring the fascination with aliens and UFOs into popular culture in subsequent years. The conspiracy theories that surround the event continue to be a source of contention even today.

The notion that life from another dimension may exist in the universe has intrigued mankind for ages. But only after the advancements in science and technology after

World War II could we think about this in any credence or scientific basis.

Since then, discussion regarding alien-related encounters with humans continue to be discussed within the scientific community as well as popular media outlets and even within social circles. A lot of people point to"the "Roswell incident" as the primary evidence or an influence on these theories.

Shortly: While there are many unknowns about what actually transpired in Roswell over a decade back, the incident is crucial. It was it a matter of weather balloons, or mysterious objects, it has captured our imaginations about possible visits or communication with other intelligent species in the time-space continuum that extends beyond the universe we know.

Background and Context

The incident occurred at a time when there was increased fascination with UFOs within the United States. It was the result of Kenneth

Arnold's observation of nine mysterious flying objects at a staggering speed over Mount Rainier on June 24 the 24th of June, 1947. This triggered a surge of interest about sightings all over America in this time. It sparked curiosity since it was believed to be credible due to Arnold's reputed credibility among other pilots.

The events that occurred around Roswell were an extremely crucial time in American time. But, Americans were still anxious due to increasing tensions between the former allies like Russia having nuclear weapons.

Allies turned adversaries following World War II, bringing new challenges to political leaders at a level that was never before seen.

The post-World World War II as well as the Cold War eras saw concerns concerning national security as well as potential threat from abroad dominating public discussion. These prompted questions regarding the development of new technology and capabilities for military inside the US administration and also among the private sector. In the context of this history, there was a fascination for reports of mysterious floating objects that appeared to be defying any explanation.

A chronology of incidents

It began early July 1947, after a devastating storm struck New Mexico. The storm caused significant damage to homes and properties across the state including the Foster ranch, which was located outside of Roswell.

In the same evening, a the local farmer W.W. "Mac" Brazel found strangely shaped debris on his property. The area covered by the debris was that was not larger than 2 to three hundred yards the diameter. At first, Brazel thought it might have been leftover debris from a number of unsuccessful weather balloons. They were launching close by the military authorities.

After securing certain samples and then bringing them to Roswell to be examined more closely, Brazel became increasingly convinced that they were a mystery. Brazel was concerned that they might be part of something more mystical. After hearing about the findings of Brazel via Mac himself, as well as the civilian authorities at Roswell, Chamberlain & Daily Record journalist J.B Fowler sought to obtain an official response by the Colonel William Blanchard of the military base.

Colonel Blanchard promptly released a press release to announce the team's recovery of the "flying disc."

It was later amended to clarify it was part an air balloon. The change was made following additional inquiries continued as a result of the increasing public attention to this story originally released by major media outlets like The New York Times and Life Magazine.

The implications of this alleged explanation provided by the government pose a number of questions. For those that believe in UFOs and intelligent life outside our planet (or perhaps parallel universes) doubt how the technology would have not been created here, given that Blair made clear in his explanation.

After initial reports of UFO sightings with a rare appearance, more evidence was discovered alongside statements that cited supposed explanations given by officials of the government at different places around town. Some examples include crash dummies being dropped by high-altitude aircrafts and statements acknowledging the lack of details about UFOs contained in official news statements. The public's skepticism increased throughout the days following.

Although it appeared as an unintentional change to the official narrative, many did not accept the different narrative. They speculated on anything from cover-ups by the government to the possibility of interplanetary diplomacy and even secret military tests on unknown devices. Media attention and public interest continued to be strong over the next months and weeks. The result was greater debates on extraterrestrial life as well as our spaceship.

Chapter 23: Witnesses And Their Accounts

Mac Brazel's story was published in an article published after his passing. Mac Brazel said he first thought the findings were bizarre however he dismissed it as a strange part of crashed aircrafts or perhaps meteorite shards. He contacted authorities and reported small beams of metallic appearance that resembled the tin foil, with different designs and hieroglyphs.

Jesse Marcel Sr.'s report from years later talked of how awed he was at first observing Mac Brazel's discoveries on Foster Ranch. Notes were dragged across his face, reflecting on the wonder of it all before calling superior officers to request for their immediate attendance. He further mentioned that the deceased residents were confronted with pieces of art in a way that was unusually.

There are reports that other people on location were also involved in the operation to recover. In particular Sergeant Melvin Brown experienced firsthand examining material found at Brazel's ranch. They twisted and formed bizarre circles, or even creases that were uncommon in typical metal alloys put under extreme stress, bending without understanding, then resuming their former shape once they have been loosened. There are reports of parts that may be different alloy. But, with no further research the validity of these claims true is yet to be verified.

The Official Explanation and Controversies Despite the initial reaction from officials in the military about the mysterious destruction, the military officials changed explanations over time.

The critics of the government's explanations to the matter point the numerous inconsistencies that exist within official reports on the incidents that took place over the two days. There is no explanation for these inconsistencies regardless of whether top-secret guidelines are followed, and no conclusion will satisfy the many people who claim that there was the government was hiding something from.

They claim that the cover-up was fabricated on the people with the intention of protecting classified information and the implications of this saga grew into the practices of government that were encased in alarming ideologies primarily linked to paranoia in this Cold War era.

Despite efforts to explain these incidents, the inconceivable origins of the claims cast doubt when examining the whole UFO phenomenon.

The skepticism that is presented here is considered factually regardless of one's personal convictions. The conclusions drawn from skepticism and independent research can be crucial in developing the ability to critically analyze and an openness to truth and obscure realities.

With technological advances continuing to advance towards exploring space, some concerns about the existence of extraterrestrial intelligence existing need to be answered. Today, we have more reason than ever before to investigate this issue seriously and consider the possibility of further exploration. It also encourages to reflect on the current state of our species now, in a world of unknown territory and the possibility of alien civilizations.

If the claims are confirmed as true the result would be revolutionary with widespread acceptance as well as optimism for looking into the universe together.

The Mantell UFO Case: A Puzzling Mid-20th Century Aerial Encounter (1948)

The Mantell UFO incident is among of the most famous instances of flying objects that are not identified as such encounters. The case dates to January 7, 1948 and was the death of a National Guard pilot who died in pursuit of the sightings he believed were the spacecraft of an alien. This article explores the case's significance in the context of mid-twentieth-century UFO sightings.

The post-war period brought forth several reports on unknown flying objects, also known as "flying saucers." In the late 1940s to mid-to-late 1950, these sightings led to an enormous fascination with ufology, and later its significance on the security of our nation within government agencies including Project Sign (which transformed into Project Blue Book), which was regarded as to be the official US Government investigation agency that investigated UFOs'. It was the 7th of January The location is Muhlenberg County, Kentucky. The principal figures in the incident included Thomas F. Mantell (25-year-old ex-wartime WWII combat vet), Alvin Gentry (45-year-old WW2 combat veteran) and Clarence Chiles (27-year-old also with prior military experience).

Around 1 pm on the 7th of January, three individuals reported seeing an odd phenomena from their position in the Fort Knox army base located Ine some miles to the east to Louisville, KY. The men described the phenomenon as having "a blue border around it" along with "white lighting" visible beneath. The incident spread widely throughout the personnel, before it was discovered by a fellow officer located at Godman Army Airfield, only 6 miles from the airfield. They said they saw an object that was oblong hovering over their heads around 20 thousand feet. Then, shortly afterward two aircrafts of the fighter jets were dispatched for observation responses. General J.F Gordon - Fort Knox's Commanding officer- received a message saying that an UFO had been observed nearby and sent fighter planes out to search for the object.

Lieutenant Colonel Thomas F. Mantell led one of the aircrafts along with the pilots he was with, Alvin Gentry and Clarence Chiles from the second aircraft when they started following. Just after taking off, Mantell radioed ground control that he had seen an object off in the distance but was unable to figure out the object. Each man was pursuing the unidentified craft around 25k feet in altitude- determined to find it Gentry was eventually unable to continue after having issues with his oxygen apparatus, and only Mantel left Fort Knox airfield pursuing the flying saucer by himself. Mantel's gas reserves were dwindling as he increased his chase distances, and possibly beyond the limits of his pursuit on his own. But he would not give up despite being directed by ground control personnel to stop because another adjustment could put Mantel at risk above the limits of any reasonable threshold.

However, he chose to go after it relentlessly by describing via radio the metallic object that was emitting vibrant beams that caused enthusiasm among those who followed every activity on the open frequencies by using Ham radios. Unfortunately, as per the US Air Force, after reaching the height of 25,000 feet (7,600 meters), Mantell went out due to the lack of oxygen. His plane started spiralling back to the ground. Witnesses later reported seeing Mantell's Mustang in a circle. Mantell's plane exploded on an agricultural property to the south of Franklin near the Kentucky-Tennessee border. The body of Mantell was recovered from the wreckage by rescue workers. The seat belt of his was torn and his watch read 3:08 p.m. that was the time that he was struck.

At 3:50 p.m. The people in Godman Army Airfield had lost sight of UFOs.

Skyhook balloons were the most popular explanation for atmospheric phenomena. One popular conspiracy theory suggests that there's more to it than what is apparent. The intelligence establishment cannot trust them due to their silence regarding this particular incident, particularly in the context of the increased cold war period suspicions that Soviets may have something to hide that could be a breakthrough in weaponry development. This is why some people refer to the incident 'The Kentucky Incident' rather than simply another case of UFO sightings.

The value of assertions like these that are backed by an open public debate attracts interest primarily due to the state's cover-ups regarding the lengthy inquiry, in addition to the publicity hype surrounding aerial phenomena which spans several decades. This sparked debates about extraterrestrial existence and opened the way for more instances to surface which further ignited curiosity about the subject.

The McMinnville UFO Photographs: A Pivotal Event in Ufology (1950)

The McMinnville UFO images are two iconic images taken created by Paul Trent and Evelyn Trent in 1950, which show an unidentified flying Object that hovers over their farm.

McMinnville, Oregon, was considered to be a rural area that was not the military's maneuvers and airports that were easily observed.

The images have captured the attention of generations of skeptics, ufologists as well as ordinary people by their mysterious and mysterious information.

The story began on the morning of May 11th, 1950 the day Paul Trent, a humble farmer from McMinnville, Oregon, grabbed his camera in order to document what he observed.

In the sky over his farm was a strange disc-shaped, circular object that was to forever alter the way he lived. Paul Trent maintained he saw an object of metallic descent to between 100 and 150 feet, before it re-emerged at an angle of about. His wife snapped both photos by using his camera.